NC 20-

ROME'S HISTORIC CHURCHES

San Giovanni a Porta Latina

ROME'S HISTORIC CHURCHES

Lilian Gunton

London
GEORGE ALLEN & UNWIN LTD
RUSKIN HOUSE · MUSEUM STREET

FIRST PUBLISHED IN 1969

This book is copyright under the Berne Convention. All rights reserved. Apart from any fair dealing for the purpose of private study, research, criticism or review, as permitted under the Copyright Act, 1956, no part of this publication may be reproduced, stored in a retrieval system, or transmitted, in any form or by any means, electronic, electrical, chemical, mechanical, optical, photocopying, recording or otherwise, without the prior permission of the copyright owner. Enquiries should be addressed to the Publishers.

© *George Allen and Unwin Ltd 1969*

SBN 04 726001 7

PRINTED IN GREAT BRITAIN
in 11 pt. Linotype Times, 1 pt. leaded
BY WESTERN PRINTING SERVICES LTD
BRISTOL

ACKNOWLEDGEMENTS

My grateful thanks are due in special measure to Rev. Cuthbert Smith, M.A., late of the Collegio Beda, Rome: Professor J. M. C. Toynbee, D.Phil., F.S.A., and Mr. John Frost for their constructive criticisms and generous sharing of specialized knowledge.

I also wish to record the courteous help given me on many occasions by the late Mgr. Giulio Belvederi of the Pontifico Istituto di Archeologia Cristiana, when I was studying in Rome.

Further to the above, I wish to express my gratitude to those many authors (some of whose names are in the bibliography) from whose life-work I have quarried so much needed knowledge in compiling my compendium of these churches all of which, although known personally to me, could not have revealed their histories without research into the profound studies which it has been my privilege to probe. The Bee gathers nectar far and wide without which there would be no honey!

Lilian Gunton

'It is generally accepted today that in Early Christian Art the purely formal elements were subordinated to the content of the works. In Architecture, this was the liturgy and the general needs of a religious community; in representational art, it was the message. Therefore, the understanding of these works depends not just on the analysis of their form, but on a correct appreciation of their basic ideas.'

    F. Van Der Meer, *Early Christian Art*, 1967

CONTENTS

	page
ACKNOWLEDGEMENTS	ix
GLOSSARY OF TECHNICAL TERMS	xx
MAP OF THE STATIONAL CHURCHES	xxv
INTRODUCTION	xxvii

The Churches

Santa Sabina	1
San Giorgio in Velabro	8
SS. Giovanni e Paolo	11
Sant' Agostino	17
San Giovanni in Laterano	20
San Pietro in Vincoli	30
Sant' Anastasia	35
Santa Maria Maggiore	37
San Lorenzo in Panisperna	43
Santi Apostoli	46
St Peter's Basilica	49
Santa Maria in Domnica	60
San Clemente	63
Santa Balbina	71
Santa Cecilia	74
Santa Maria in Trastevere	78
San Vitale	84
SS. Marcellino e Pietro	88
San Lorenzo fuori le Mura	91
San Marco	95
Santa Pudenziana	100
Sant' Agata dei Goti	104
San Sisto Vecchio	107
SS. Cosma e Damiano	110
San Lorenzo in Lucina	113

CONTENTS

Santa Susanna	117
Santa Croce in Gerusalemme	120
SS. Quattro Coronati	125
San Lorenzo in Damaso	130
San Paolo fuori le Mura	132
San Martini ai Monti	138
Sant' Eusebio	142
San Nicolo in Carcere	144
San Crisogono	148
Santa Maria in Via Lata	151
San Marcello al Corso	155
Sant' Apollinare	159
Santa Francesa Romana	162
Santo Stefano Rotondo	167
San Giovanni a Porta Latina	170
Santa Prassede	174
Santa Prisca	177
BIBLIOGRAPHY	181
SOURCES OF ILLUSTRATIONS	184
INDEX OF ARCHITECTS AND ARTISTS	187
INDEX OF SAINTS	189
INDEX OF CHURCHES	191

ILLUSTRATIONS

Plates

FRONTISPIECE	San Giovanni a Porta Latina		
1	Santa Sabina	*facing page*	18
2	San Giorgio in Velabro		19
3	SS. Giovanni e Paolo		26
4	San Giovanni in Laterano		26
5	Santa Balbina		27
	Sant' Anastasia		27
6	Santa Maria Maggiore		28
7	San Pietro in Vaticano		34
8	San Pietro in Vaticano		35
	Santa Maria in Domnica		35
9	Santa Maria in Domnica		66
10	San Clemente		67
11	Santa Maria in Trastevere		74
12	Santa Cecilia		74
13	Santa Maria in Trastevere		75
	Santa Cecilia		75
14	San Vitale		75
15	SS. Marcellino e Pietro		82
	San Sisto Vecchio		82
16	San Lorenzo fuori le Mura		83
17	San Marco		114
18	Santa Pudenziana		115
19	SS. Cosma e Damiano		122
20	San Lorenzo in Lucina		122
	Santa Susanna		122
21	Santa Croce in Gerusalemme		123
	San Martino ai Monti		123
22	SS. Quattro Coronati		123
23	San Paolo fuori le Mura		130
24	San Crisogono		131
	San Nicolo in Carcere		131
25	San Crisogono		162
	Santa Francesca Romana		162

ILLUSTRATIONS

26	Santa Maria in Via Lata	163
	San Marcello al Corso	163
27	Santa Prisca	170
28	San Giovanni a Porta Latina	171
29	Santa Francesca Romana	178
30	Santa Prassede	179
	Santo Stefano Rotondo	179

Text figures

Fig. 1	The Stational Churches	*page* xxv
Fig. 2	Santa Sabina	2
Fig. 3	SS. Giovanni e Paolo	12
Fig. 4	San Giovanni in Laterano	22
Fig. 5	San Pietro in Vincoli	31
Fig. 6	Santa Maria Maggiore	38
Figs. 7–10	St Peter's Basilica	50, 52, 54, 56
Figs. 11–12	San Clemente	64, 66
Fig. 13	Santa Maria in Trastevere	80
Fig. 14	San Marco	96
Fig. 15	Santa Pudenziana	102
Fig. 16	San Lorenzo in Lucina	114
Fig. 17	Santa Croce in Gerusalemme	123
Fig. 18	SS. Quattro Coronati	126
Figs. 19–20	San Paolo fuori le Mura	134, 136
Fig. 21	San Nicolo in Carcere	145
Fig. 22	Santa Maria in Via Lata	152
Fig. 23	San Marcello al Corso	156
Fig. 24	Santa Francesa Romana	164

ORDER IN WHICH THE STATIONAL CHURCHES ARE VISITED

Santa Sabina	Ash Wednesday
San Giorgio in Velabro	Thursday following
SS. Giovanni e Paolo	Friday following
Sant' Agostino	Saturday following

First Week in Lent

San Giovanni in Laterano	Sunday
San Pietro in Vincoli	Monday
Sant' Anastasia	Tuesday
Santa Maria Maggiore	Wednesday
San Lorenzo in Panisperna	Thursday
Santi Apostoli	Friday
St Peter's Basilica	Saturday

Second Week

Santa Maria in Domnica	Sunday
San Clemente	Monday
Santa Balbina	Tuesday
Santa Cecilia	Wednesday
Santa Maria in Trastevere	Thursday
San Vitale	Friday
SS. Marcellino e Pietro	Saturday

THE STATIONAL CHURCHES

Third Week

San Lorenzo fuori le Mura	Sunday
San Marco	Monday
Santa Pudenziana	Tuesday
Sant' Agata dei Goti	Tuesday
San Sisto Vecchio	Wednesday
SS. Cosma e Damiano	Thursday
San Lorenzo in Lucina	Friday
Santa Susanna	Saturday

Fourth Week

Santa Croce in Gerusalemme	Sunday
SS. Quattro Coronati	Monday
San Lorenzo in Damaso	Tuesday
San Paolo fuori le Mura	Wednesday
San Martino ai Monti	Thursday
Sant' Eusebio	Friday
San Nicolo in Carcere	Saturday

Passion Week

San Pietro in Vaticano	Sunday
San Crisogono	Monday
Santa Maria in Via Lata	Tuesday
San Marcello al Corso	Wednesday
Sant' Apollinare	Thursday
Santa Francesa Romana	Thursday
Santo Stefano Rotondo	Friday
San Giovanni a Porta Latina	Saturday

THE STATIONAL CHURCHES
Holy Week

San Giovanni in Laterano	Palm Sunday
Santa Prassede	Monday in Holy Week
Santa Prisca	Tuesday
Santa Maria Maggiore	Wednesday
San Giovanni in Laterano	Thursday
Santa Croce	Friday
San Giovanni in Laterano	Saturday
Santa Maria Maggiore	Easter Sunday

GLOSSARY OF TECHNICAL TERMS

Absiodoles   Secondary apses terminating the side aisles in churches.

Aediculum   A niched recess. Generally decorated with small columns supporting some kind of gable or tympanum.

Ambones   Marble pulpits one on either side of the nave for the reading of the gospel and epistle respectively.

Annular crypt   A crypt in the form of a passage following the inside curve of the apse.

Apse   Semi-circular or polygonal recess, arched or dome-roofed, especially in a church.

Architrave   Horizontal unit supported on columns.

Atrium   Courtyard often with arcades placed before the main entrance to a building.

Baldachin or *baldacchino*   A canopy suspended or supported upon pillars above the high altar.

Basilica   In its basic features, an oblong hall terminating in an apse, with two or four longitudinal arcades—or sometimes colonnades—supporting the nave walls. The term is often used loosely in connexion with Christian churches, since the norm permitted of considerable variation in detail as, for instance, the introduction of a transept.

Campanile   A bell-tower. The term is not generally used of Norman or Gothic towers unless they stand detached from the church.

Cancelli   Railings of bronze or other metal.

Coffered ceiling   Sunk panels in a ceiling.

Columbarium   A building whose inside walls are hollowed out in niches to hold urns containing the ashes of the cremated dead. So called from its likeness to a dovecot.

GLOSSARY OF TECHNICAL TERMS

Conch — A semi-dome over a semi-circular apse.

Confessio — English *confession*. The space immediately below or more often in front of the high altar in a church.

Cornice — Ornamental moulding on a wall.

Cosmatesque work — Roundels of coloured marbles, serpentine, and porphyry, laid down on church floors. These coloured marbles and stone are also in borders of white marble on vertical surfaces such as panels on pulpits and altar-frontals, together with glass mosaic in gold and colours.

Crypt — Underground vault, especially one beneath a church.

Diaconiae — Charitable institutions of the Church dispensing corn, etc., after or during, the failure of the Roman imperial doles. Normally attached to a church in busy centres.

Dominicum — The earliest Christian assemblies for religious worship were in private houses, i.e. the *ecclesiae domesticae*. Whence the name *dominicum* or *domus Dei*, the Lord's house.

Ecclesia — Can either mean (a) the assembly of the people or (b) the place of assembly; thus, in both senses: church.

Fresco — A painting made on a wall or a ceiling before the plaster is dry.

Loculus — A wall-grave in a catacomb.

Matroneum — A gallery for the women of a congregation.

Mensa — A table. The altar-table in a church.

Narthex — A colonnade or an arcade across the façade of a church. In some cases this is inside the building, the aisles being returned across the door end thus forming an inner narthex called the eso-narthex.

Opus sectile — Marble cut into sections, often roundels cut from a column used on floors in churches.

Pediment — Triangular part crowning the front of a building.

Pendentive — Spherical triangles formed by intersection of dome

GLOSSARY OF TECHNICAL TERMS

by two pairs of opposite arches springing from the four supporting columns.

Plutei — Screens of pierced marble enclosing the sanctuary or the choir.

Portico — A roof supported by columns, or arches, usually attached as a porch to a building.

Schola cantorum — The enclosure for the choir, at the head of the nave.

Spandrel — Space between adjoining arches and the moulding above.

Stational church — Derived from *statio* which originally was a local term indicating the place where a particular administration was situated, e.g. *statio annonae*, a market. Taking a more military significance it passed to the designation of a barrack where a corps of guards were on duty also during the night, and with this sense it passed into ecclesiastical language. Thus *statio* could indicate the place and the ceremony in which and with which the anniversary of a martyr's death was kept, passing the night in prayer or in watching. *Statio* came to be applied to the procession headed by the pope which moved from one church to another, called the *station*, the church in which the holy sacrifice of the Eucharist was to be offered.

Titulus — Actual meaning in antiquity, a nameplate used on a house or on a tomb-chamber. In Christian usage the *tituli* were parish churches called by the name of the founder, man or woman, before the introduction of dedicating churches in the names of the saints, e.g. the *titulus Equitii*; the *titulus Vestinae*, etc.

When the pope creates a cardinal he gives him a special jurisdiction over a parish church in Rome, in which the cardinal is said to 'take his title'. Thus, Cardinal Heenan takes his title in the church of San Silvestro-in-capite, in Rome.

GLOSSARY OF TECHNICAL TERMS

Transennae   Pierced metal slabs used to mark the enclosure in front of the confession or of the sanctuary.
Transept   Transverse part of a cruciform church.
Travertine   A porous light-yellow rock.
Tympanum   The space, often triangular, over a door between the lintel and arch.
Volute   Spiral scroll characteristic of Ionic, Corinthian and Composite capitals.

KEY TO MAP OF STATIONAL CHURCHES

1 Sant' Anastasia
2 Sant' Apollinare
3 Santi Apostoli
4 Santa Balbina
5 Santa Cecilia
6 San Crisogono
7 San Clemente
8 SS. Cosma e Damiano
9 SS. Quattro Coronati
10 Santa Croce in Gerusalemme
11 Santa Maria in Via Lata
12 Santo Stefano Rotondo
13 Sant' Eusebio
14 San Giorgio in Velabro
15 San Giovanni in Laterano
16 SS. Giovanni e Paolo
17 San Giovanni a Porta Latina
18 San Lorenzo fuori le Mura
19 San Lorenzo in Damaso
20 San Lorenzo in Lucina
21 San Lorenzo in Panisperna
22 San Marco
23 San Marcello al Corso
24 SS. Pietro e Marcellino
25 Santa Maria in Domnica
26 Santa Maria Maggiore
27 Santa Maria ad Martyres
28 Santa Maria in Trastevere
29 San Nicolo in Carcere
30 SS. Nereo ed Achilleo
31 San Paolo fuori le Mura
32 San Pancrazio fuori le Mura
33 St Peter's Basilica
34 San Pietro in Vincoli
35 Santa Prassede
36 Santa Prisca
37 Santa Pudenziana
38 Santa Sabina
39 Santa Susanna
40 San Martino ai Monti
41 Sant' Agostino
42 San Vitale
43 San Sisto Vecchio
44 Sant' Agatha
45 Santa Francesca Romana

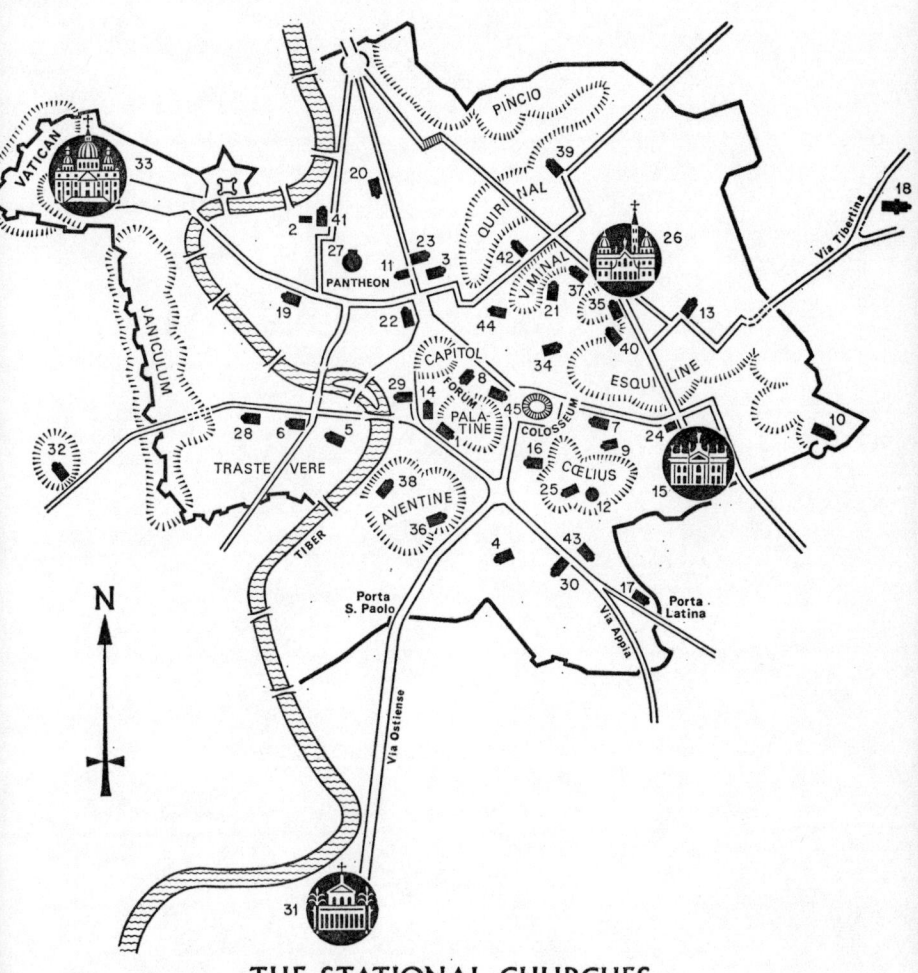

THE STATIONAL CHURCHES

Fig. 1

INTRODUCTION

This book is concerned with those churches in Rome, all of ancient origin, that are known as Stational Churches. These vignettes follow the liturgical sequence in which they are visited in rotation during the season of Lent.

In the early days Christians had to congregate for worship in private houses where a sufficiently large room could be provided. By the third century they had come into possession of communal properties for their cult, but as these were liable to be confiscated by the pagan authorities (and often suffered that fate) they still had the appearance on the outside of ordinary dwelling houses.

With the advent of political tolerance under the Emperor Constantine the Great all confiscated properties were restored to the Christians and church building went ahead at an astonishing pace.

The cathedral-church of the Lateran and the memorial basilicas of St Peter on the Vatican Hill and of St Paul on the road to Ostia were paid for from imperial funds but the parish churches were provided by the generosity of private citizens. These were called *tituli* (titles) and bore the names of their benefactors, e.g. a church close to the modern Via Nazionale was called the *titulus Vestinae* because it was built with money left in her will for that purpose by a Roman lady named *Vestina*.

As the fifth century advanced these personal titles began to be replaced by the names of saints. One of the first to receive a patron saint was Vestina's church, for when Pope Innocent I (401–17) came to dedicate it he placed it under the protection of St Vitalis, the martyred bishop of Ravenna.

Some of the parish churches were built into the foundations of the houses in which Christians had assembled during the

INTRODUCTION

persecutions; others stand above the traditional homes of local martyrs.

Early in the sixth century a practice arose of making interparochial visitations in Lent. The procedure commenced with the members of the different parishes meeting together at a prenamed church (called the *collecta*) and then with their priests walking in procession, led by the Pope, to a further church, there to attend a communal service. The idea was to prevent the parishes, scattered around the city, from becoming isolated one from another.

This was called 'making the stations', an appellation derived from the Latin word *statio*, indicating a place where a particular administration was situated. For example, a *statio annonae* was a market place. It then passed into military use, meaning a barracks with guards continually on duty and finally came into ecclesiastical parlance.

This Lenten practice continued throughout the centuries—with a break in continuity in the later Middle Ages—and is very much alive today; receiving fresh impetus from Pope John XXIII's enthusiasm in leading the processions on Ash Wednesday to the church of Santa Sabina on the Aventine Hill, to which the station had been allocated by Pope Gregory the Great (590–604). Pope Paul has continued the practice.

On their days stational churches are decorated with flowers and evergreens and set out on view their treasures, chalices, reliquaries, etc. Masses are offered in the morning and processions chanting litanies take place in the afternoons, with an atmosphere of joy prevailing. These churches are filled with history and contain, like the sands in an hour-glass, the movement of Time bound within their walls.

To give a few examples. The early-twelfth-century church of San Clemente stands above its fourth-century predecessor whose foundations are in a house of the first century and of a mithraeum of the third century. Here one literally walks on history. In Santa Maria in Trastevere one era is so blended with another that the centuries visibly 'hold hands'. In Santa Croce in Gerusalemme, where relics of Christ's Passion are

INTRODUCTION

preserved, those pivots of history, Constantine and his mother, St Helena, come alive again at the sight of the earth from the Holy Land brought to Rome in St Helena's baggage-train.

It is the purpose, then, of this book to help those visiting Rome and those lacking the opportunity to walk her streets to enjoy some of the less-known beauties of that most complex and fascinating city.

SANTA SABINA
Aventine

Pope Gregory the Great (590–604) fixed the order of the churches in which the 'station' was to be held in Lent. After the ashes had been distributed in the church of Sant' Anastasia, at the foot of the Palatine Hill, the Pope with the clergy of the different parishes and their congregations walked in procession to attend Mass in the church of Santa Sabina on the crown of the Aventine. The distance to be covered was considerable, ending in a stiffish climb, and in later years the Pope and the cardinals traversed it in the saddle, which explains the existence of a ramp at Santa Sabina in place of the customary flight of steps.

How the Church Gained its Name
In the early centuries churches were not dedicated in the names of the saints but were known by those of their founders, cleric or lay, and prefaced by the word *titulus*. In the beginning of the fifth century the *titulus Sabinae* was built in honour of a Roman lady, Sabina, who during the days of the persecutions had established a private chapel in her home on the Aventine for the congregating of local Christians. Rooms of the second-century house, believed to have been hers, still exist beneath the nave. Whether Sabina suffered death for the Faith has been a disputed point, but by the sixth century her church had become the *titulus sanctae Sabinae*. Whatever the true facts, the church has known no other title.

Architecture and Decoration
Architecturally, this is considered the finest existing example of an early Christian basilica. Built between 425 and 432, its

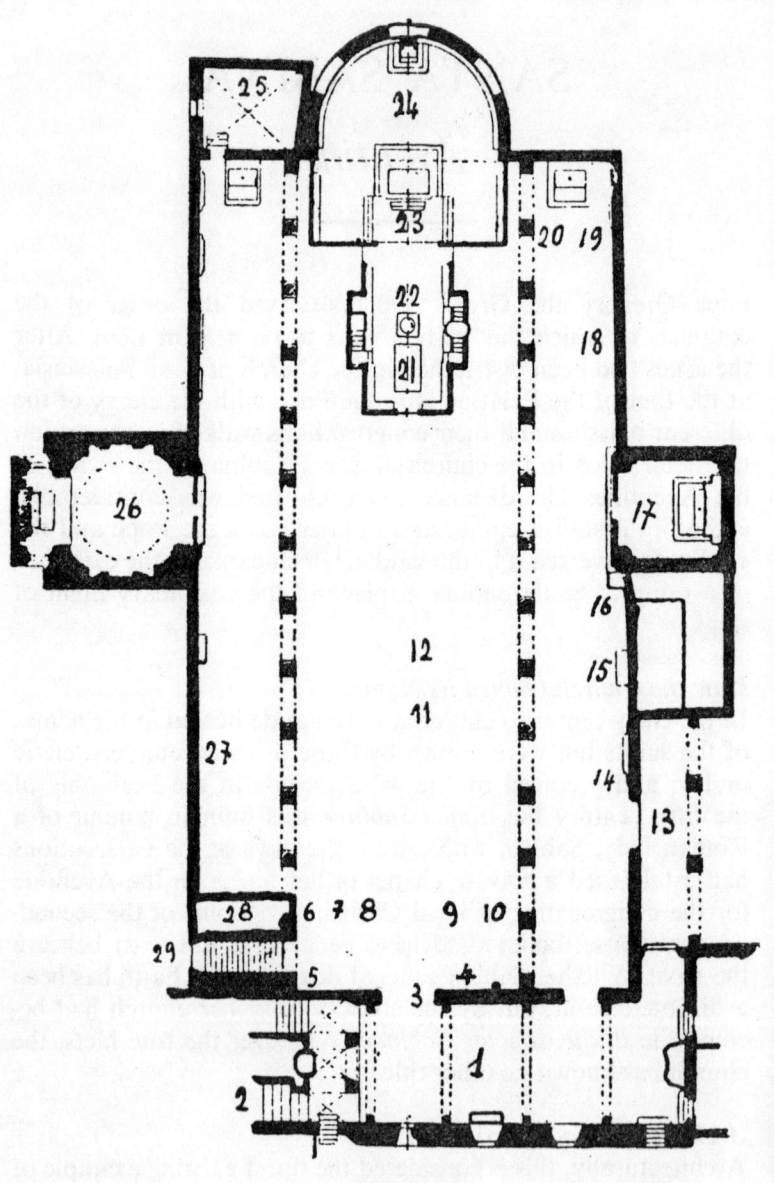

Fig. 2

exterior of warm Roman brick is characteristically unostentatious, and despite the wear and tear of the centuries the plan and the fabric are substantially unchanged. The long portico that covers the lower half of the façade was originally one side of an enclosed *atrium*, now become part of the monastery garden. Of the portico's three doors, two have survived, but the church is now entered from the bottom of the right-hand aisle.

The interior gives the satisfaction of defined space that is both harmonious in proportion and perfectly adapted to its purpose; the wide nave stretching to the sanctuary uninterrupted by a transept, in true basilican style.

Authorities differ as to the provenance of the white marble columns, supporting arcades, that enclose the aisles. Professor Muñoz, who skilfully restored the building, considered that they were made for the purpose; others think it more probable that they were re-used from some classical source.

The handsome circular-headed windows have been reopened and filled with a transparent mica set into geometric designs copied from ninth-century fragments which were found in the bricked-up recesses of the frames. Of the marbles with which the walls were adorned, only those in the spandrels of the arches remain.

The Basilica's Early Treasures
Of the basilica's early treasures two have survived *in situ*: the

---

Fig. 2

Santa Sabina
1. Portico (A.D. 425–32).
3. Sculptured cypress-wood door. Early fifth century.
4. Remains (*avanzi*) of a Roman house.
12. The mosaic tombstone (unique of its genre) of Fra Muñoz da Zamora, died March 7, 1300.
13. Entrance to the church from the nave.
17. Chapel of St Hyacinth.
21. Choir enclosure. Reconstructed, including panels from the original *schola cantorum*.
23. Papal altar, enclosing relics of the saints.
24. Bishop's throne (*cathedra*).
26. Chapel of St. Catherine of Sienna.

famous cypress-wood door in the portico and the long mosaic inscription that surmounts the door on the inner side.

The carvings on the door illustrate episodes from the Old and the New Testaments. While some are similar in iconography and in technique to Roman sarcophagi of the third and fourth centuries, others show Eastern influence, in content and in form.

One beautiful panel of the latter class depicts a woman standing in prayer between St Peter and St Paul, who mutually hold what appears to be a crown above her head. This symbolizes the universal Church located in the visible world, for the figures have above them the sun and the moon and the arch of heaven, in accordance with the cosmological belief of the time. In the upper zone of the panel Christ stands in glory holding a scroll with the mystical fish, the *Icthys*, inscribed upon it.

At the top of the door, on the left-hand side, is the earliest-known representation of the Crucifixion. It is unrealistic in conception for Christ and the thieves are standing upon the ground before what appears to be a brick wall, to which their hands are irregularly nailed. Here the two traditions are mingled: that of the West in that Christ wears only the loincloth; that of the East in that he is bearded.

The Mosaic Inscription

The mosaic inscription, in beautiful lettering upon a blue ground, informs the reader that the church was erected during the pontificate of Pope Celestine I (422–32), at the expense of an Illyrian priest 'One worthy to bear the name of Peter'. At either end stands a darkly robed female figure of great dignity. Beneath the feet of the one are the words ECCLESIA EX CIRCUMSIONE and beneath the other ECCLESIA EX GENTIBUS. These symbolize the two parts of the universal Church: that of the Jews, and that of the Gentiles.

The eminent medievalist, Emile Mâle, once wrote that he could never look at these stately figures without recalling two splendid Christian women, Marcella and her adopted daughter Principia, friends of St Jerome, who had to flee from their burning house on the Aventine to take refuge in the basilica of St Paul out on the road to Ostia on that night of terror, August 24th, A.D. 410, when Rome fell to the Gothic invaders under Alaric.[1]

Historical Events
Too numerous to recall are all the historical events that crowd the past of this grand church. One of enduring import occurred when Pope Honorius III (1216–27) gave it and part of his adjoining private palace to St Dominic who made it the headquarters of his new Order of Friar Preachers. This entailed some constructional alterations since the church was a parochial one, with a baptistery. St Dominic is said to have 'followed the example of Solomon' and ordered the nave to be cut into two portions, reserving the sanctuary end for his Community.

A cloister was a necessary addition, one side being partitioned into sections to serve as studies where manuscripts could be copied or illuminated. It was in one of these semi-open cells that St Thomas Aquinas wrote part of his *Summa*. (The cloister at Gloucester cathedral is a surviving example of this character.)

When Henry of Luxembourg sequestered the property in 1312, the Dominicans moved into Rome to their newly erected church of Santa Maria Sopra Minerva. But connection with their home on the Aventine was not severed, although more than once interrupted with violence.

The monastery at Santa Sabina came to be a favourite resort of the popes, especially in time of carnival. Pope St Pius V (1566–72) loved its comparative remoteness and added a wing from the upper story of which a glimpse might be had into the garden, where a cross between billiards and bowls is sometimes enjoyed at recreation.

With the vigorous Pope Sixtus V (1585–90) came activities good, and less good. His architect Fontana demolished the

[1] Emile Mâle, *Rome et ses vieilles églises.*

dividing wall in the nave of the basilica and so restored the plan, but he also banished the choir-enclosure and other marble furnishings and bricked up all but three of the windows on either side of the nave. The existing choir is modern and plain but some of the medieval slabs are inserted in it.

In 1882 there came another confiscation and the civil authorities 'took over' the cloisters and the monastery and made them into a hospital. Bought back at a high price from Mussolini's government, all is once more in Dominican hands, with the proviso that the church and the cloisters are classed as a national monument. If this occasions some inconvenience, it also helps with the expense of upkeep. Fortunately the attempt made to remove the cypress-wood door and place it in a museum failed.

Points of Interest
In a recess beneath the altar is a small sarcophagus which contains a lead casket embossed with Pope Sixtus V's coat-of-arms. Within the casket are reputed relics of 'Saint Sabina' and of her Christian slave, 'Saint' Serapia; together with relics of three authenticated martyrs, Alexander, Theodulus and Eventius, priests put to death under the Emperor Hadrian. These had been brought into the church by Pope Eugenius II (824–27), as recorded in his existing epitaph.

When the floor of the nave was relaid in 1936 parts of a thirteenth-century paving were uncovered together with tombstones, inscriptions and an effigy in mosaic of Marico di Zamora, General of the Dominicans, who died in 1300. This effigy is unique of its genre in Rome and has been inserted in the new floor.

The minute cell of St Dominic can be visited and has preserved its austere simplicity although it is now entered through an ante-chamber elaborately adorned by Borromini. This chamber contains the armorial bearings of the Bourbon, Charles IV, who redeemed the monastery in 1815 from one of its confiscations and gave it back to the Community.

Another cell, that of Pope St Pius V, has been made into a

chapel where hangs his portrait and the beautiful ivory crucifix before which he so often knelt in prayer.

In the garden flourishes a descendant (a cutting from a cutting) of the orange tree brought from Spain by St Dominic. From the fruit of the original tree St Catherine of Sienna made a gift of five candied oranges to Pope Urban VI. With the seeds of the oranges, the Friars make excellent rosaries. Such were originally reserved for popes and cardinals, but it is now, on occasion, possible to obtain one.

A painting by Il Sassoferrato (G. B. Salvi), depicting the Virgin handing a rosary to St Dominic, is in the church. St Catherine of Sienna is included in the picture and to her the Babe on his mother's knee gives with his right hand a rosary and with his left hand sets upon her head a crown of thorns.

SAN GIORGIO IN VELABRO
Via San Giorgio

In contrast to the church of Santa Sabina, that of St George 'in Velabro' is situated at the foot of the Aventine Hill. *Velabrum* was the name of a lake, or marsh, formed in antiquity by the overflowing of the Tiber, for near by was the quay where corn from Africa was disembarked. When Byzantine influence was strong in Rome a large Greek colony dwelt in the district. It was a busy, noisy region surrounding a cattle market which advertised its character with the statue of a bronze bull. Today it is still an individual, picturesque quarter much beloved by artists.

Approaching the church from the piazza with the intriguing name, Bocca della Verità (Mouth of Truth), the visitor leaves on his right-hand side the charming church of Santa Maria in Cosmedin, built partly into the ruins of a temple of Ceres, goddess of corn, and passes a four-faced arch popularly called the Arch of Janus. This was erected in the fourth century and has in its upper section a room where the public scribes and the money-changers carried on their business.

The origin of San Giorgio is obscure and there is little recorded about it until the statement in the *Liber Pontificalis* that Pope Leo II (681–83) built the existing fabric. That he built upon an older foundation is indicated by the irregular plan, narrowing from the entrance to the apse.

Restorations took place under Pope Gregory IV (827–44), but owing partly to the inundations it was not long before it fell into decay and neglect; as was the fate of many of the smaller city churches between the ninth century and the eleventh.

Architectural Features
The aspect of the exterior dates from the early twelfth century at which time it was brought into line with the late-medieval

fashion and received its architraved portico and its sturdy belltower. This was inserted, not to say squeezed, into the corner of the left-hand aisle, with an outer side adjoining the Arch of the Argentarii, silversmiths and cattle dealers who raised it, according to the inscription, in honour of the imperial family of Septimus Severus.

As these brick bell-towers are one of the charming features of the Roman scene and part-and-parcel of Romanesque churches a short commentary is not out of place.

Rising in arcaded stories to differing heights, they are often independent structures yet they follow no set rule. Many stand against the wall of the nave flush with the façade. At the church of SS. Quattro Coronati, the tower surmounts the gateway that led into the *atrium*. Others stand bravely above Baroque façades like forgotten sentinels holding the centuries at bay.

The Interior
The interior retains its irregular, seventh-century form and its ancient columns culled from pagan sources. Those on the left-hand side have Corinthian capitals; those on the right have two Corinthian, four Ionic, and two crude imitations of Ionic with uncarved volutes.

To the careful restorations of Professor Muñoz, who swept away much accumulated lumber, is owing the satisfying simplicity that now prevails. The windows in the apse and those in the nave were reopened and filled with a golden selenite set into geometric patterns, in conformity with the medieval style. When the sunshine filters through the selenite, it tempers the coldness of the stone walls and brings to prominence the fine twelfth-century canopy above the altar in the small sanctuary.

The Saints of the Dedication
Pope Leo dedicated his church in the names of St George and St Sebastian, thus uniting the Greek and the Latin loyalties in a way not unusual at that period. The cult of St George had come to Rome with the Byzantine armies and after Belisarius, Justinian's general, had repaired the city walls he set the names

of the two warrior saints above the gate that opens to the Via Appia, now called the Porta San Sebastiano.

St Sebastian was a Roman soldier attached to the court of Diocletian. He is believed to have suffered a double martyrdom, his arrow-pierced body being finally flung into a public sewer from which it was retrieved and buried in a catacomb on the Via Appia.

In the eighth century Pope Zachary (741-52), who like St George was a native of Cappadocia, gave the major relic of the Saint's skull to the church and from that time the name of St Sebastian as co-patron died out. The skull is preserved in a reliquary beneath the altar.

The Fresco in the Apse
In the vault of the apse is a fresco, much repainted, of which the original has been assigned alternatively to Cavallini or to Giotto. This probably replaces an earlier mosaic that portrayed the same theme. In the centre of the composition the tall figure of Christ stands upon a mount with the Virgin and St George on the one side and St Peter and St Sebastian on the other. Owing, presumably, to the tradition that St George was the patron saint of cavalry as with the passing of time he became that of knighthood and chivalry, he is accompanied by his white horse. The dragon of his legend, now so familiar in art, had not yet made its début!

St Sebastian's features and his clothing resemble those in a seventh-century icon in the church of San Pietro in Vincoli, where he is depicted as of mature age, as became his military rank, and carrying his sword and his shield. A different conception from that of the handsome youth whose naked torso bristles with arrows, so beloved of Renaissance artists.

The church is now in the care of a Dutch Community residing at 19 Via San Giorgio (adjoining the church), where application for admission may be made when the gate is locked.

It is of interest to English pilgrims that Cardinal Newman took his title in the Sacred College from San Giorgio in Velabro.

SS. GIOVANNI E PAOLO
Caelian Hill

The fascinating church of St John and St Paul is by no means unique in being founded upon the house of the titular saints, but the events concerning their death and burial are exceptional for they took place in that awkward interval, the reign of Julian the Apostate.

According to the tradition, Saints John and Paul were brothers, or friends, who had been attached to the imperial court but who had offended Julian by their refusal, on religious grounds, to enter his service. As their public execution would have been a highly controversial act an officer was sent to behead them in their own home, and their bodies were buried beneath the house, hurriedly and secretly. Such, in brief, is the account based upon a late document called their 'Passion', which some authorities consider to be wholly spurious while others, equally eminent, hold to be basically historical. Whatever the true facts of the martyrdom, a church was built above the house at the close of the fourth century and the place became a popular bourne of pilgrims up to the tenth century, as testified in the Itineraries and by the Christian paintings upon the subterranean walls. After that time the house was sealed off from the church as being structurally unsafe, and so remained until its discovery in 1877.

The House on the Caelian Hill
In imperial times the south-east side of the Caelian Hill lay, strictly speaking, outside the city boundaries. On this 'majestic and isolated' incline a large temple (the *Claudarium*) had been built, but in the second century this solitary locality began to change its character. Residential possibilities came to be

Pianta della Chiesa.

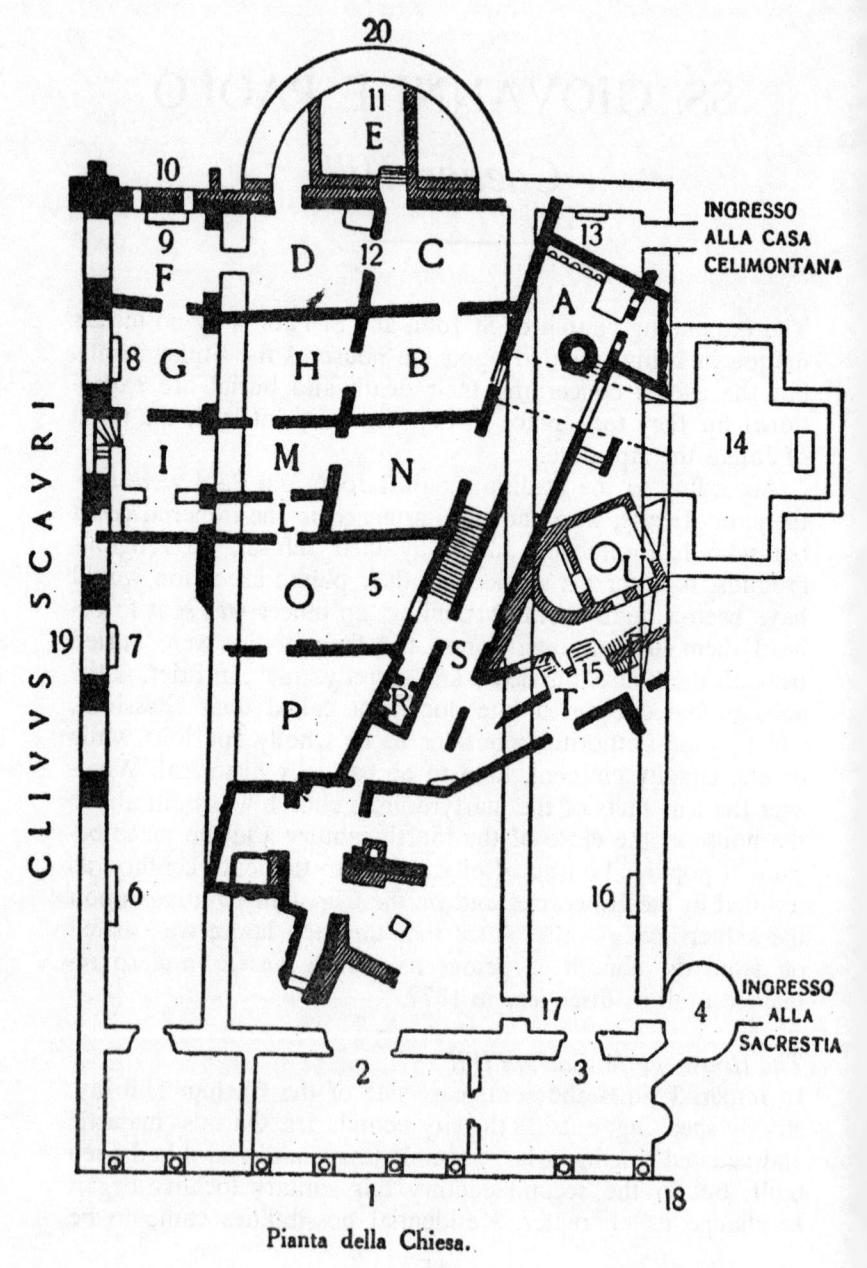

Fig. 3

considered and a middle-class house was built facing a road called the *Clivus Scauri*, which passed by the temple. This road, or lane, retains its rural aspect.

The locality developed and the first house was followed by two others, with shops beneath them, higher up the hill. One belonged to a pagan who painted his rooms with conventional scenes while the other may have belonged to a Christian family. However that was, there came a time when the two houses were made into one by an owner who overpainted the pagan fantasies with Christian themes and made structural alterations by knocking down walls to make one large room. Archaeologists call this the Room of the Orans because of a fresco depicting a figure with arms extended in the Jewish and early Christian attitude of prayer. The arrangement of the rooms and their decoration recall the interior of part of the Roman villa at Lullington, in Kent, which was so constructed for Christian assemblies.[1]

[1] J. M. C. Toynbee, *Art in Roman Britain*, 1962.

Fig. 3

SS. Giovanni e Paolo
1. Façade and portico.
2. Cosmatesque doorway, flanked by columns from the fourth-century façade.
4. Entrance to the sacristy.
9. Altar of the Blessed Sacrament.
10. Behind the altar. Fresco of Christ and Apostles, 1255.
12. High altar. Beneath it, red porphyry urn containing the relics of Saints John and Paul.
14. Chapel of St Paul of the Cross (1857–80).
15. Altar of Panamachius, founder of the church.
19. Exterior of two houses; one second century, the other third century.

Outlined in Black—the Underlying Structures
A. Courtyard—with large pagan fresco of mid-third century.
C. So-called *triclinium* (reception or dining hall). Frescoes with vine, trellis, birds etc.
I. Medieval oratory. Remains of Christian frescoes of ninth century.
N. The room now called the Room of the Orante—figure on the wall in the Christian attitude of prayer, i.e. standing with arms outstretched.
R. The shaft of the martyrs' shrine. Fourth- or early fifth-century frescoes on the inner walls.

In this house, which had become their property, Saints John and Paul were executed and buried.

The Building of the Basilica and the Shrine-Shaft

Towards the end of the century, a Catholic layman, Pammachius, son of the senator Byzantius, built a church above the house. This was not at first dedicated in the names of the martyrs, but was called the *titulus Pammachi* as named in a synod held under Pope Symmachus in 498.

A shaft was carried up from the place of burial in successive stages until its top penetrated the nave floor of the church. Upon the interior walls of the shaft are fourth, or early-fifth-century frescoes. One depicts a woman and two men with hands tied behind their backs awaiting the fall of the executioner's sword. Their identity is uncertain, but that they were connected in some way with the titular martyrs seems evident. It is possible that they were apprehended while seeking to remove the bodies of the two martyrs and give them Christian burial. It has been suggested that they were Crispus, a priest, Crispianus a deacon and Benedicta a Christian woman, all closely associated with the legend of Saints John and Paul according to the Passion.[1]

Other frescoes in the shaft are difficult to interpret but are definitely Christian in theme.

Within the decade 1950–60 this whole complex building has been scientifically explored and, assisted by the generosity of its titular-priest, the late Cardinal Spelman and of his friend, the former ambassador Joseph P. Kennedy, extensively restored and made easy and safe of access.

The Present Aspect of the Basilica

The upper part of the façade has now been cleared of obscuring brickwork. The enclosed gallery beneath the arcading dates from the thirteenth century. The portico is a reconstruction of

---

[1] A. Prandi and G. Ferrari, *The Basilica of Saints John and Paul on the Caelian Hill*, 1958.

the one erected by Pope Adrian IV (Nicholas Brakespeare), the only English pope. The campanile was originally free-standing, its lower part raised upon one of the bays of the *Claudianum*. The upper, later and more elegant sections have twin arcaded openings on each of the four sides.

It was the custom with medieval craftsmen to inset ceramic bowls and plates into the bell-towers, to catch and reflect the rays of the sun. Those in the tower of SS. Giovanni e Paolo were amongst the most beautiful, brought from Malaga in Spain where they were painted and glazed. One bowl is twelve inches in diameter and has a black pattern upon a green ground encircled with blessings and salutations in Arabic. These precious ceramics have been removed and are now in a small museum, near to the sacristy. Glazed terracotta copies have been set into the tower.

The Interior of the Church
The interior of the church has seen no less changes than the exterior; in fact rather more. The ancient columns in the nave are concealed within heavy pilasters and the side aisles have been filled with a series of chapels. All that is visible of the medieval period are portions of the pavement and part of a fine fresco showing Christ with six of the Apostles, each figure standing in an arcaded frame.

In the right-hand aisle is a commemoration of Pammachius, the Founder. This is a painting by Milani and shows the 'Saint' holding the plan of his church. He had married Pauline, daughter of St Paula, and after his wife's death he spent his days in the service of the poor. At Ostia he built a hospice for strangers where he attended the sick with his own hands. When he died in 410, St Jerome composed his panegyric.

The Chapel of St Paul of the Cross
In the same aisle is the entrance to the handsome chapel of St Paul of the Cross, founder of the Passionists, whose incorrupt body lies beneath the altar. Born at Ovada in north Italy in 1649, St Paul learned through a series of visions that he was

called at the age of twenty-six to found a Congregation especially devoted to Christ's Passion. Although he never left Italy, he was deeply concerned about the conversion of England. 'England is always before my eyes, and if ever it becomes Catholic the benefit to the Church will be immeasurable.'

More than a century later his spiritual son, Dominic Barberi, mystically inherited this love for England and as is well known was instrumental in the conversion and the reception into the Church of John Henry Newman. The recent beatification of Barberi by Pope Paul VI has recalled the immensity of his labours and of the sufferings he so devotedly endured. He has been called 'The father of modern ecumenism' and in his dealings with controversial issues was far in advance of his time.

The Underlying House
From the sanctuary end of the same aisle a stair descends into the underlying regions. In the first room to be entered a fourth-century stair led to the area where a tiny cemetery of three or four graves has been discovered in the recent researches. The adjoining and larger room was in its pagan era an open court embellished with a fountain and a large painting. The Christian owners plastered this over but it has been partially uncovered and the colours are still bright and well-preserved. Three central figures are surrounded with a maritime background. Their identity is still debated. The suggestion that the scene represents the marriage of Thetis, mother of Achilles, seems probable.

To the right-hand side of the fresco is a block of masonry bearing a Christian monogram and the aspiration: *Rufine vivas* (Rufinus may you live) 'in Christ' being understood, as in the catacomb inscriptions.

From this room rises the shaft described above. In other rooms are fragments of Christian paintings including one of the Crucifixion. Another shows the soldiers dicing for Christ's seamless coat.

SANT' AGOSTINO
Piazza di S. Agostino

The history of the existing church of Saint Augustine of Hippo (to which the Lenten Station was transferred after the destruction of the church of St Trypho) unrolls to a mere five centuries. Rather surprisingly, there had been no church in Rome in honour of this great saint until in the late fourteenth century the Austin Friars (Augustinians) built one for themselves on a site 'not far from the Field of Mars'.

This modest edifice was replaced by Cardinal d'Estouteville, Protector of the Order, with one of the finest churches of the Early Renaissance. The Cardinal's architect, Baccio Pontelli (builder of the Sistine Chapel), did not pull down the whole of the earlier building but cleverly converted the nave and sanctuary into the transept whose exterior apsidal wall with its attractive fourteenth-century cornice can be seen from a side street, the Via del Pianellari. The rebuilding dates from 1480.

Architectural Features and Works of Art

Borrowings from ancient monuments were still possible at the time and it is said that the wide flight of steps in front of the façade were constructed with blocks of travertine from the Colosseum.

The interior of the basilica is impressive both in height and solidity. The cupola over the sanctuary excited contemporary comment since it was unique at that date in Rome with a window at the summit like the Cyclopean Eye of the Pantheon.

Notable amongst the many works of art are Il Guercino's[1] painting of St Augustine, in the right-hand transept; a fresco of

---

[1] So called because he squinted. Real name Giovanni Barbieri.

the Prophet Isaiah, high on the third pilaster on the left-hand side of the nave attributed (controversially) to Raphael; and the venerated statue of La Madonna del Parto, surrounded by ex-votos expressing gratitude for safety in childbirth.

As regards Raphael's painting of Isaiah, Georgio Vasari felt no doubts. Before Michelangelo had completed his stupendous fresco on the vault of the Sistine Chapel (about which he was more than usually anxious as to secrecy) he was temporarily absent from Rome and Bramante, architect of the new St Peter's, took Raphael by night to inspect it. Vasari writes: 'Bramante had the keys of the chapel and being friendly with Raphael he showed him Michelangelo's methods so that he might understand them. This at once led Raphael to do over again the Prophet Isaiah in Sant' Agostino. Aided by what he had seen of Michelangelo he greatly increased the figure, endowing it with majesty. When Michelangelo saw it afterwards he concluded that Bramante had played him this bad turn to benefit Raphael.'[1]

Sacred Relics and the Tomb of St Monica

When St Trypho's church was taken down, relics of saints preserved there were moved to Sant' Agostino and beneath the altar lie those of St Trypho, martyred at Nicaea under Decius, and of St Respicius who was converted by witnessing the other's fortitude.

The most treasured possession of the basilica is the tomb of St Monica, mother of St Augustine. It had been the first concern of the Friars when they built their own church to bring to it her body from Ostia where she had died and been buried. This they had done 'with ceremony and joy'.

It cannot be doubted that Monica's admonition to her son: 'Lay this body anywhere, be not concerned about that; the only thing I ask of you is that wheresoever you are, you make remembrance of me at the altar of the Lord' was faithfully

---

[1] Giorgio Vasari, *The Lives of the Painters, Sculptors and Architects*.

Church of Santa Sabina
Built between A.D. 423–430. The narrow Roman bricks have not parted company with their mortar in fifteen hundred years.

Church of Santa Sabina
A panel from the cypress-wood main door. Christ giving sight to the blind (*top*), the miracle of the loaves and fishes (*centre*), the marriage at Cana (*below*).

Church of Santa Sabina
The dignified female figure holding an open book symbolizes the Jewish side of the Universal Church. Her counterpart, representing the Gentiles, stands at the other end of the Latin inscription that surmounts the inside of the main door.

The Church of San Giorg[io] in Velabro

Seventh-century nav[e], Romanesque tower a[nd] portico.

The Church of San Giorg[io] in Velabro

The medieval fresco in [the] apse includes St Geo[rge] with his white horse. [Be]neath the altar is the re[lic] of the Saint's skull.

SANT' AGOSTINO

observed by St Augustine and his spiritual sons have tenderly cared for her body. It lies now in a splendid sarcophagus of *verde antico* beneath the altar of the Blessed Sacrament, at the head of the left-hand aisle.

A propos the internment at Ostia, an important memento came to light in 1945 when two boys preparing some ground for a game, accidentally dug up part of St Monica's tombstone with its inscription by *Anicius Bassus*. (R. Meiggo, *Roman Ostia*, Clarendon Press.)

SAN GIOVANNI IN LATERANO
Piazza San Giovanni

The first Sunday in Lent holds its station in the Lateran Basilica, Rome's cathedral, 'Mother and Head of the churches in the city and in the world', as the inscription on the pediment proudly proclaims. The station is also held here on Palm Sunday and on the Wednesday and Friday in Holy Week.

Constantine the Great dedicated this, his first church, to Christ the Saviour. It was not until the twelfth century that the name of St John the Baptist began to supersede in popular usage the correct title. As to the appellation 'in Laterano', that derived from the Roman family of the Laterani who originally owned the land.

Emile Mâle[1] made the comment that to enjoy these ancient churches 'some little history is necessary'. For none is that dictum more true than for the Lateran. To many who enter it for the first time it appears to be a demonstrative example of the late Baroque, paradoxically rather chilling in atmosphere and quite remote from its own past. Actually, despite the heavy burden of the centuries and the drastic changes imposed upon the venerable fabric, it enshrines a rich inheritance of Christian teaching restated in a different medium (but not destroyed) and when that is understood the emotive thermometer rises.

Constantine's Basilica
Constantine's basilica was approached through a porticoed *atrium* and entered by five doors that pierced the lower half of the façade. Upon the upper part was a mosaic image of Christ with those of the four major prophets.

[1] Emile Mâle, *Rome et ses vieilles églises.*

SAN GIOVANNI IN LATERANO

The nave was flanked by double aisles, of which the inner pair had white marble columns supporting an arcading while the outer pair had smaller columns of a beautiful green basalt. Above the arcading a series of mosaic panels illustrated themes from the Old and the New Testaments. Twelve Prophets stood in a line above the Old Testament themes facing the Twelve Apostles on the opposite side. The disposition formed a concordance the purpose of which was to show how the Mosaic Law found fulfilment in the Christian Law and that the expected Messiah was Jesus Christ. This was a method of instruction familiar in the early Church, but depicted here for the first time in monumental art.[1]

When the English abbot, Benedict Biscop, was paying one of his visits to Rome in the seventh century he saw these mosaics in the Lateran and called them *Imagines ratione compositas* (well-conceived images) and upon returning to England he had a similar series arranged in his monastic church at Jarrow.

In the semi-dome of the apse a beautiful mosaic illustrated a radiant and profoundly theological conception of the Blessed Trinity participating in the Baptism of Christ, represented in a medallion at the junction of the arms of a cross set upon Mount Zion.

This precious monument is in the existing apse but has suffered two important changes. At some period the Hand of God the Father coming forth from the clouds of heaven above the bust of Christ the Son was replaced by a chorus of cherubim and this disrupted the theme of the Trinity. The second alteration can be dated with precision since it took place under the first Franciscan pope, Nicholas IV (1288–92), at the hands of his artists, Fra Jacobus and Fra Torriti. As first conceived, the figures of the Virgin Mother, St Peter and St Paul stood with raised hands venerating the cross on one side and St John the Baptist and St John the Evangelist and St Andrew in the same attitude, on the other side. The Franciscan artists, filled with

[1] J. Wilpert, *Rivista di Archeologia Cristiana*, 1929, Nos I and II.

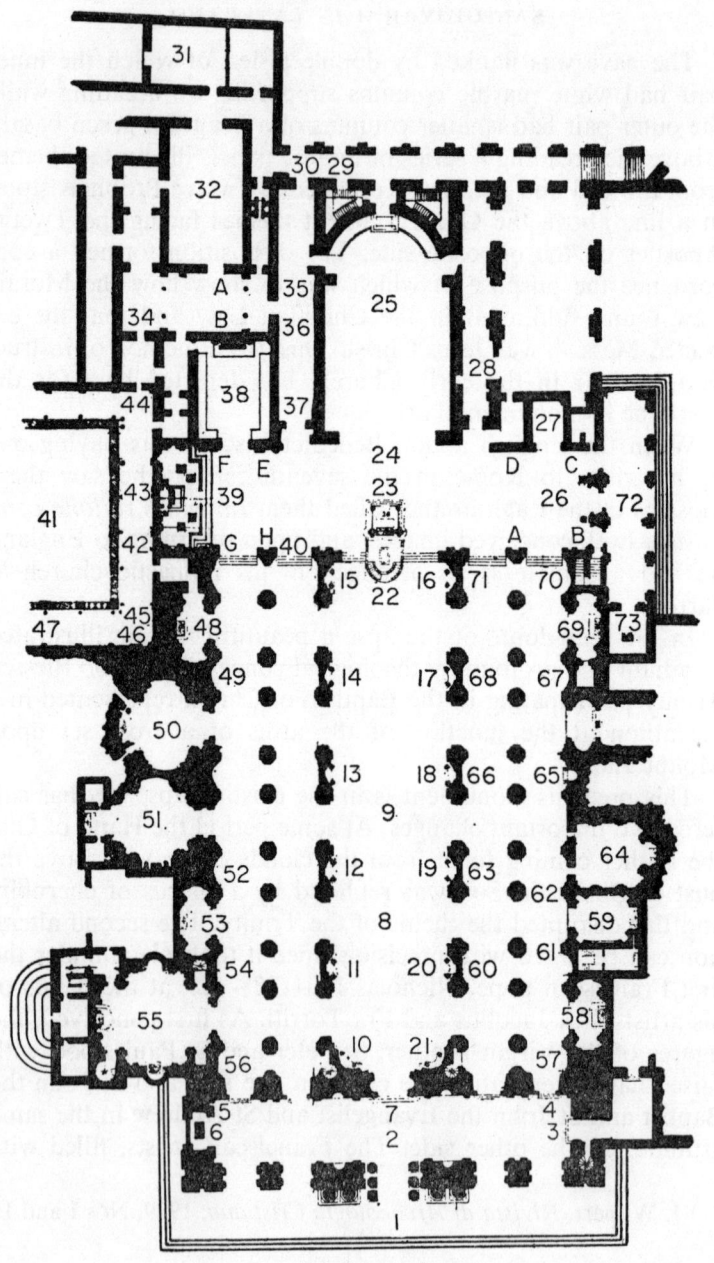

Pianta di S. Giovanni in Laterano.
Fig. 4

fraternal zeal, squeezed in St Francis of Assisi between Our Lady and St Peter and St Anthony of Padua between the Baptist and the Evangelist. Moreover, they brought down Our Lady's hand from its correct position to place it upon the tiara of Pope Nicholas, seen kneeling at her feet.

The Baptistery

It was customary for many centuries for baptisteries, 'the gateways into the Faith', to be independent buildings. Constantine's baptistery was rectangular and comparatively small but was replaced in the fifth century by the existing octagon opening to two small side-chapels. Pope John IV (640–42) added a larger chapel to house the relics of his compatriot, St Venantius, and those of other Dalmatian martyrs conveyed to Rome. He set their life-size portraits, in mosaic, upon the side walls of the apse each with his name above his head. The Virgin with hands raised in intercessory prayer stands between St Peter and St Paul beneath the bust of Christ in the centre of the apse.

For its iconographic importance and study of ecclesiastical vestments this chapel is well worth visiting.

The Baptismal Rite

Baptism was administered by partial immersion, the neophytes stepping down into a sunken font provided with a raised partition for the officiating priest, normally the bishop. The

---

Fig. 4
San Giovanni in Laterano
 2. Entrance portico, the work of Galilei (1732–35).
 4. Porta Santa, the holy door used in jubilee years.
 8. The interior refashioned by F. Borromini.
10–21. Pilasters, enclosing the ancient columns—and statues of the Apostles.
23. Papal altar.
25. The apse, remade in 1886, incorporating the ancient mosaic.
29. Statues of Saints Peter and Paul.
39. Altar of the Blessed Sacrament.
41. Cloisters, 1215–32.
60. Giotto's fresco, brought from the *loggia* of the old palace.
72. The *loggia* for benedictions and north façade constructed by Fontana (1585).

ceremony has been evocatively described as practised in the time of St Augustine of Hippo (circa 400):

'The moment was one of intense solemnity. Silence would fall as, surrounded by the packed throng, a priest (it may have been St Augustine himself) consecrated the water making over it the sign of the cross and saying a prayer to God and Christ "that he might condescend to cleanse the element of water of all evil, sanctifying it and endowing it with divine power for this element of water receives its cleansing power through the sufferings of Christ".

'The candidates now remove all their clothing; loose their hair and remove their girdles. Not a hairpin must remain on the head, not an earring on the ear nor a ring on the finger nor an amulet around the neck. They enter the mystical womb of their Mother the Church as they have come out of that of their earthly mother.

'There is no embarrassment for they have all been accustomed from childhood to the freedom practised in the baths. . . . The men stand on one side, the women on the other, the latter being assisted by the deaconesses and older women. Under the light of the lamps one after the other passes through the curtains which have been slightly withdrawn and descends the steps into the streaming water, the subdeacons and godfathers lending a hand. First come the children, then the men. The women come last of all. The person being baptized must, as St Augustine points out "Step downwards, for participation in the sufferings of the Lord demands humility".'[1]

At the conclusion, the new Christians were clothed in white; received the sacrament of confirmation and finally, standing together apart from the congregation, were admitted to the central mystery of the Faith, Holy Communion.

The Scala Santa (Holy Stairs)
An historical event occurred for the Lateran when the Empress-Mother, St Helena, brought home from the Holy Land

[1] F. Van der Meer, *Augustine the Bishop*.

the marble stairs traditionally venerated as those ascended by Christ at his trial before Pilate. The stairs were set up close to the basilica, but later on were moved to the medieval chapel of St Lawrence, now called the *Sancta Sanctorum* on account of the many precious relics preserved beneath the altar.

The Lateran Palace

As the Lateran Basilica was Rome's cathedral an episcopal residence was required and Constantine gave the palace of the Laterani to the bishop (Pope Miltiades (311–14)) and for the next millennium that was the official home of the papacy. It expanded gradually into a vast straggling complex surrounded by a protecting wall guarded by a fortress-tower in which Pope Zacharius I (741–52) caused to be painted the maps of the Christian world.

A *triclinium* (reception-cum-dining hall) was added to the palace by Pope Leo III (795–816), to commemorate the crowning of Charlemagne as Emperor of the West on Christmas Day in the year 800. In the apsidal recess in this hall Leo put a mosaic in which he introduced a portrait of Charlemagne and one of himself, both wearing the rectangular halo signifying that it was executed in their mutual life-time. A copy of this mosaic is now on a concave wall built for the purpose upon the site of the *triclinium*. This isolated monument sometimes puzzles those who notice it since its *raison d'être* is not self-evident.

The Jubilee Year of Thirteen Hundred

Roughly parallel to the *triclinium* ran the long Hall of the Councils where so many ecclesiastical assemblies were held, including five Ecumenical Councils. From the open-air loggia at the north end of the Hall papal benedictions were given and it was there that Pope Boniface VIII proclaimed the Jubilee Year of 1300. It is said that while Giotto was still a pupil of Cimabue's he was summoned to Rome by Pope Boniface and given the commission to depict His Holiness proclaiming the Jubilee. Giotto painted the scene upon an inner wall of the loggia and when that was pulled down his fresco was detached from the wall and is now (under glass) on a pilaster in the Lateran basilica.

The Jubilee marked the peak of prosperity for the Lateran and its dependencies, so long the hub of papal and monastic and pilgrim activities. When the popes departed for Avignon the blight of neglect settled over the whole city and after their return the papal residence was established in the healthier air of the Vatican Hill. But this move did not disrupt the liturgical life of the cathedral.

Restoration and Decoration of the Basilica

Under Pope Martin V (1417–31) careful restorations were started and a new floor was laid in the nave with marbles collected from disused city churches. Martin was a member of the aristocratic family of the Colonna and in the design of his floor are incorporated groups of feigned columns.

A complete redecoration of the walls was also undertaken. The mosaic panels of the concordance of biblical themes had been cracked during an earthquake in the ninth century. The then-reigning pontiff, Sergius II (844–47), could not afford so costly a medium, but had the same episodes copied in fresco. After the passage of five hundred years these were probably in bad condition, or considered to be old-fashioned, and Pope Martin had the walls replastered and painted anew with scenes from the lives of St John the Baptist and St John the Evangelist.

The Lateran Palace is Pulled Down

History now goes forward to the days of Pope Sixtus V (1585–90), an enthusiastic and virile if not an artistic builder. After demolishing the octopus-like palace of the Lateran, he built the existing, very much smaller one. The loggia of the papal benedictions was replaced by the two-storied porch in front of the north transept of the basilica. Opposite this porch (the usual entrance to the church) stands a granite obelisk that had been brought by one of the emperors from Heliopolis. Pope Sixtus, who was addicted to moving obelisks, placed it there to fill the gap after the removal of a famous bronze equestrian group

SS. Giovanni e Paolo
Fifth-century nave. Eleventh-century porch. The cupola of the Chapel of St Paul of the Cross, nineteenth century.

SS. Giovanni e Paolo
Shaft connecting the martyrs' tomb-place with the nave of the church.

SS. Giovanni e Paolo
One of the fifth-century frescoes on the inside walls of the shaft. Depicts the donors of the fresco venerating one of the martyrs.

San Giovanni in Laterano
Borromini's reconstruction of the nave and his rearrangement of the figures of the ancient concordance.

San Giovanni in Laterano
The re-set apsidal mosaic with the thirteenth-century alterations.

Santa Balbina
Fifth-century building. Windows restored to their ninth-century form and style.

Sant' Anastasia
Seventeenth-century façade—fronting the fifth-century church.

Santa Maria Maggiore
Built by Pope Sixtus III (432–440). Enclosed by the palace that Pope Benedict XIV built in 1741.

Santa Maria Maggiore
Apsidal mosaic of the Coronation of the Virgin —thirteenth century.

Santa Maria Maggiore
Detail of the apsidal mosaic. The stigmata can be seen on St Francis' hand.

which had graced the spot for centuries in the belief that the rider of the horse was Constantine the Great. When it was discovered that he was Marcus Aurelius the group was taken by Michelangelo to form the centre-piece of his newly arranged piazza on the Capitol.

Borromini Refashions the Basilica

The next major change came under Pope Innocent X (1644–55) and his great achitect, Borromini. The Jubilee Year of 1650 was approaching and the Pope desired to embellish his cathedral. Borromini planned to pull down the whole edifice and to rebuild in the fashionable Baroque style, but Pope Innocent did not agree. He wished to preserve as much as possible of the structure and also, surprisingly, to have the figures and the biblical themes of the concordance restored to the nave. Such a wish had been rendered possible by the researches of an archaeologist, Abbot Albani, who had discovered that Pope Sergius' ninth-century frescoes were still discernible beneath the fifteenth-century plaster and he was able to decipher most of the episodes.

The Concordance Re-dressed

The Pope's request could not be ignored but Borromini, who was much more interested in converting a medieval church into a Baroque one, arranged the components of the concordance to suit his architectural scheme, and the proper sequence was consequently disrupted. At the head of his vast pilasters, six on either side of the nave, six prophets painted upon canvas face six prophets on the opposite wall. All are wrapt in meditation or write upon their scrolls, seemingly oblivious of the twelve Apostles far below in the nave, whose super life-size statues stand within canopies, of which the forward-curving pediments rest upon Constantine's green basalt columns, removed from the inner aisles.

The biblical histories, executed in stucco, are midway upon the pilasters. Whether Benedict Biscop would call these dramatic and figure-filled compositions *Imagines ratione compositas* is open to question. Certainly the concluding pair, where Jonas retreats in dignified haste from the menacing jaws of a colossal sea-monster and a muscular Christ *leaps* rather than rises from the tomb, would have astonished him. Nevertheless, the remarkable (and little-known) fact remains that the ancient concordance is still in the Lateran Basilica still proclaiming, if with changed tempo, the same Catholic and Apostolic Faith.

The New Façade

In 1732, Galilei raised the handsome façade and crowned its pediment with a statue of Christ carrying his cross as a triumphal standard. Beneath Christ's feet is the Chi-Rho, the Greek monogram of his name, the sign set by Constantine upon the standard of his legions.

The Apse is Rebuilt

In 1886 came the last important alteration. The old apse was taken down and a new one sited seventy feet further back in order to enlarge the sanctuary. The mosaic in the conch was dismantled piece by piece and reset in the new apse. The bust of Christ in the upper zone had been framed originally in a travertine mould, forming an individual unit, as was customary in antiquity with specially important portraits. The Franciscan restorers had left this frame intact, but the nineteenth-century mosaicists, less erudite or less careful, discarded it and set the cubes in the ordinary way.

The Heads of St Peter and St Paul

In conclusion this 'Mother and Head of all Churches' possesses as her greatest treasure portions of the skulls of St Peter and St Paul.

Removal of the heads from the bodies of famous martyrs in order to protect them more securely had taken place before the large-scale translation of relics from the catacombs to the city churches. Pope Honorius I (625–38) is said to have removed the head of the young martyr, St Agnes, from her tomb on the Via Nomentana and to have placed it in the papal chapel in the Lateran palace. The skull of St Sebastian was at an early date taken to the crypt in the church of the SS. Quattro Coronati. Those of the Princes of the Apostles were probably transferred to the Lateran Palace in the ninth century. They were certainly there in the eleventh. On Easter Monday in the year 1370 Pope Urban V moved them from the palace to the basilica, where they were enshrined in the lofty ciborium above the high altar where (not without vicissitudes) they have remained.

From the earliest representations in art: in the frescoes in the catacombs; on the sculptures on the sarcophagi; in the monumental mosaics in the churches, St Paul has companioned St Peter. 'Both shed their blood in Rome; Rome provided their last resting place; and from time immemorial their feast is celebrated on the same day.'[1]

The Lateran Cloisters
The cloisters of Rome are amongst the loveliest in Italy. Some date from the early twelfth century (one from the late eleventh), but the existing cloisters at the Lateran were constructed only in the first quarter of the thirteenth century, contemporary therefore with those of the Benedictine monastery at St Paul's Basilica. Both are in the fully developed 'Roman' style, architecturally, whose chief characteristics include retention of the rounded arch; great variety in design in the coupled shafts that sustain the arcades and on the friezes and capitals where the sculptured motifs reveal both fantasy and humour. With the addition of stuccoed ornament and of mosaic inlay wrought by the 'Cosmati' school brilliancy of colour completed the effect.

At the juncture of the paths in the centre of the cloisters at the Lateran stands a well-head more ancient by several centuries than its surroundings; while relics of the medieval furnishings of the basilica (not untouched with pathos as are all things material when time has discarded them) add interest to the walls.

To conclude on a practical note: cloisters are often closed at midday and not open in the afternoon; those at the Lateran close at 12.30.

[1] E. Kirchbaum, *The Tombs of St Peter and St Paul*, 1959.

SAN PIETRO IN VINCOLI
Piazza di San Pietro in Vincoli

Leaving the traffic-filled Via Cavour and ascending the steep slope of the Via San Francesco di Paolo the pilgrim finds himself (albeit breathless) in the comparative peace of a piazza high on the Esquiline Hill. Confronting him is the church of St Peter's Chains now abutting upon the modern building of the Faculty of Engineering which has blocked up the windows on the right-hand side of the nave and 'adopted' the handsome cloisters as its courtyard.

The façade is half concealed by its fifteenth-century portico whose fine wrought-iron gates are usually locked and the church is entered from the bottom of the left-hand aisle.

Architectural Features and Decoration
Upon entering it is well to pause for a moment, to adjust a first impression. 'Though often restored, it retains its original plan and columns, and is not only one of the most important remaining churches of the pre-Gothic age, but is unique in Rome in having columns of the Doric Order, whose effect is almost obliterated by the barbarous Baroque superstructure.'[1]

The Professor's stricture has reference to Francesco Fontana's elaborately coffered ceiling with its large central painting of a miracle ascribed to the Chain. But most observers will be less impacted by this incongruity than impressed by the exceptional width of the nave and the serene nobility of the whole, although it is to be regretted that the floor has recently been relaid with polished travertine.

Founded in the fourth century, the basilica had to be rebuilt

[1] A. Frothingham, *Monuments of Christian Rome*, 1925.

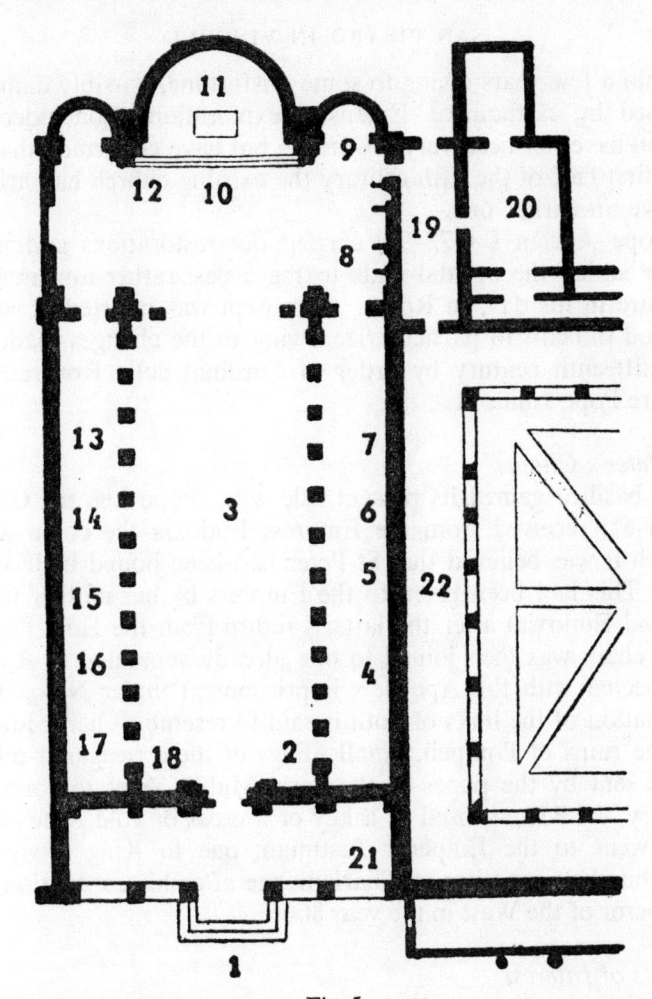

Fig. 5

San Pietro in Vincoli
1. Fifteenth-century porch. The gallery was superimposed in 1574.
3. Large central painting on the ceiling: 'The Miracle of the Chains' by G. B. Parodi.
8. Michelangelo's monument for Pope Julius II.
10. Confession before the high altar—contains the reliquary with the chains.
14. Seventh-century mosaic of St Sebastian.
18. Tomb monument with the busts of the brothers A. and P. Pollaiuolo.
20. Sacristy.
22. Cloisters, by G. da Sangallo. Now the forecourt of the modern building of the Faculty of Engineering.

SAN PIETRO IN VINCOLI

within a few years owing to some misfortune, possibly damage caused by earthquake. Extensive explorations (concluded in 1960) have not been very rewarding but have confirmed that in the first half of the fifth century the existing church had arisen above an earlier one.

Pope Adrian I (772–95) carried out restorations and may have added the apsidal ends to the aisles, rather an unusual feature in his day, in Rome. A transept was inserted at some period difficult to particularize owing to the changes made in the fifteenth century by order of Cardinal della Rovere, the future Pope Julius II.

St Peter's Chains

The basilica gained its present title when Pope Leo the Great (440–61) received from the Empress Eudoxia the chain with which it was believed that St Peter had been bound in Jerusalem. This had been given to the Empress by her mother (also named Eudoxia) after the latter's return from the Holy Land. The chain was then joined to one already venerated in Rome connected with the Apostle's imprisonment under Nero. The formation of the links of both is said to resemble chains found in the ruins of Pompeii. Small filings of these treasured relics were sent by the popes in the early Middle Ages to contemporary V.I.P.s, enclosed in a key or a cross of gold. One such gift went to the Emperor Justinian; one to King Oswy of Northumbria; another to Charlemagne after his coronation as Emperor of the West in the year 800.

Points of Interest

When the modern confession (enclosed space in front of the high altar) was under construction there came to light a fourth-century marble sarcophagus having seven compartments that contained relics of the Seven Macabees, together with a bronze plate naming the relics. Like Eudoxia's Chain they had come from the East where the Macabees had long been honoured, and St Augustine had commemorated them with the rather ambiguous phrase: '*Occisi pro lege Moyse, sed nominis Christi in lege velato*'. (Slain for the Law of Moses, yet for the name of Christ veiled under the Law?)

Above an altar in the left-hand aisle is a seventh-century mosaic of the Roman soldier, St Sebastian, similar in style to the fresco in the church of San Giorgio in Velabro, as mentioned above. When plague was raging in Rome in 680 this icon was carried in procession through the streets while prayers were offered and St Sebastian's intercession sought. The plague ceased and Pope Agatha restored the icon to the church.

Michelangelo's Statue of Moses

The attraction *par excellence* that lures innumerable visitors is the world-renowned statue of Moses. As is familiar knowledge, this was but one of the forty figures conceived by Michelangelo for a free-standing tomb for Pope Julius II that was to have been erected in St Peter's basilica. For many frustrating reasons (including the superstition awakened in the Pope's breast that by preparing his tomb he might accelerate his occupation of it!), the vast project was never completed. One reduced side was finally placed at the head of the right-hand aisle in this church because Julius had been its cardinal-titular.

'Looking tentatively at Moses, the lawgiver of Israel, as Michelangelo saw him, one realizes that the sculptor was filled with the desire to release the spirit imprisoned in a mountain by blasting and carving away the inessential. This fantastic thought came to him during his stay in the Carrara mountains where he had been several times to purchase marble for his Julian tomb. In fact, his Moses is more than a man. He is the spokesman and herald of the Ancient of Days with whom he was allowed to consort as a friend even though the Lord appeared to him hidden in the burning bush. This, and his entire life's history, his destiny and that of his chosen people are expressed in the peerless figure.'[1]

As it stands, the monument seems to express its creator's more resigned state of mind as his long and troubled life drew

[1] Rolf Schott, *Michelangelo*, 1963.

to its close. In the original conception the Moses was to have been flanked by two virile male figures, the Heroic Captive and the Dying Captive (now in the Louvre, in Paris), but these were replaced by the late-conceived contemplative figures of Rachel and of Leah.

It is perhaps not wholly inappropriate that the statue of the greatest prophet by the chisel of the greatest sculptor is found in a building dedicated to chains, awakening the reflection that the man of marble like the man of flesh was debarred from entering the Promised Land.

Pietro in Vaticano

ctuary and High Altar with Bernini's Canopy, covering the area of St Peter's Tomb-place.

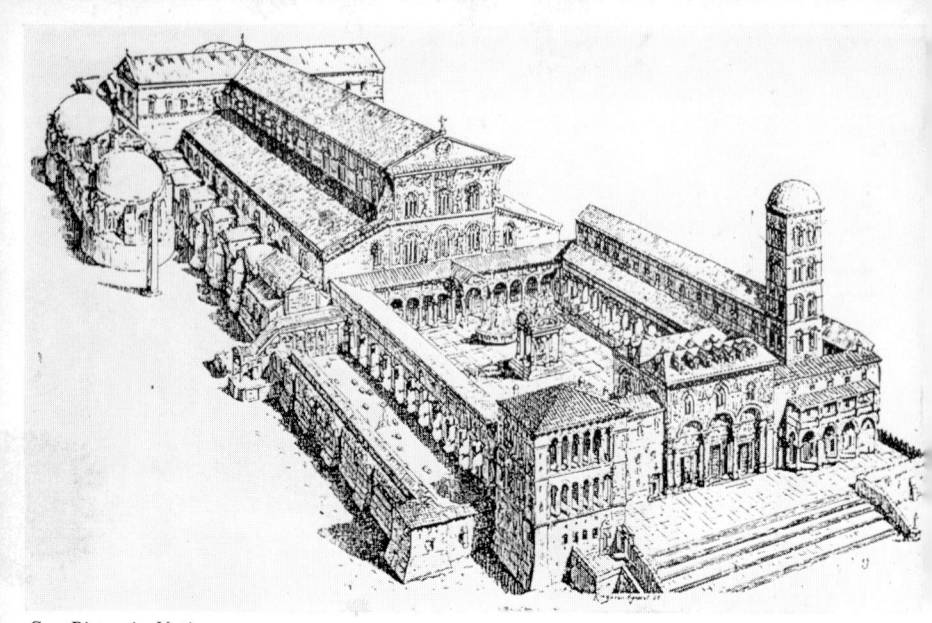

San Pietro in Vaticano
Constantine's Basilica—with later additions. The obelisk is in its original position—before moved
its present site in St Peter's Piazza.

Santa Maria in Domnica
Ninth-century nave. Early sixteenth-century portico with lions' heads in the keystones of the arc
in compliment to Pope Leo X (1513–21).

SANT' ANASTASIA
Piazza di Sant' Anastasia

At the foot of the Palatine Hill a church called the *titulus Anastasiae* had been built in the fourth century, taking its name from the foundress. It was an important building, cruciform on plan. Later, when the exarchs (viceroys of the Byzantine emperors) were in residence on the Palatine they used it as their official place of worship but changed the title to Saint Anastasia in honour of a martyr of the same name whose veneration they brought with them from the East.

St Anastasia Commemorated in the Christmas Mass
St Anastasia had suffered death by burning and her relics had been taken to Byzantium where her feast was celebrated on December 25th, the alleged date of the martyrdom. When her cult was established in Rome a commemorative prayer was inserted in the Mass which the popes sang at dawn on Christmas Day, in the exarchs' church on the Palatine. This prayer is still included in the second Christmas Mass in the Latin Rite but the Greeks now keep St Anastasia's feast on December 22nd.

The church is one of the largest in Rome and stands withdrawn in a quiet piazza, maintaining, despite the vagaries of style that have affected it, an aristocratic austerity that might fancifully be likened to that of a noble family who have acquiesced in modernization while remaining conscious of their lineage.

Structural Changes
The first big structural change took place under Pope Leo III (795–816), who, wishing to bring the plan into conformity with

SANT' ANASTASIA

that of a contemporary Roman basilica, added side aisles to the cruciform nave. Eight centuries later Pope Urban VIII raised the existing façade with its pleasing twin towers and in 1721 the Baroque architect, Carlo Gimach, refashioned the interior.

The central doorway now opens to an inner narthex which adds to the dignity of the magnificent nave. The aisles were not deprived of their ancient columns but received the exceptional arrangement of alternating arched and rectangular openings, the whole surmounted by an elegant cornice. The impressive ceiling has its counterpart in the handsome marble floor, from whose level three broad steps rise to the sanctuary with its forward-standing altar. Beneath the altar is a shrine within which the effigy of Saint Anastasia lies with her head resting upon a pillow of faggots, with reference to her ordeal and death by fire. An early fresco portrait of the Saint wearing the headdress of a dedicated virgin is extant in the crypt of the church of St Chrysogonus, with whom her history was traditionally linked.

Summing up impressions of this noble fane it may be said that it remains a *milieu* where shades of the cultured and colourful Byzantines could still feel at home.

SANTA MARIA MAGGIORE
Esquiline Hill

Of the numerous churches built in honour of Mary, Mother of God, the earliest in the West was that erected by Pope Liberius (352–66), on the Esquiline Hill, in Rome. According to the legend, the Queen of Heaven personally communicated to the Pope her wish for the church and on August 5th, in the year 358, the site was found marked out by a fall of snow. This church was called the Liberian Basilica.

The Rebuilding of the Basilica in the Fifth Century
Liberius' comparatively small edifice was replaced by the existing magnificent one by Pope Sixtus III (432–440), who made use of much of the same materials. The rebuilding was undertaken as an act of thanksgiving after the Council of Ephesus had condemned the heresy of Nestorius who denied that Mary was truly *Theokotos*, truly the Mother of God, but only the mother of Christ's human personality. This second church was called Santa Maria Maggiore: the Greater Church of St Mary.

The nave of Sixtus' basilica is now concealed, like a jewel within a casket, by the papal palace built around it by Pope Benedict XIV in 1741. At the same time the existing medieval façade was enclosed by a galleried portico. The Romanesque tower is topped by the small steeple imposed upon it (steeples are 'foreign' to Roman architecture) by Pope Gregory XI (1370–78), after his arrival in Rome from Avignon.

The Grand Interior
Very different is the grand interior, tranquil with the integrity and unity of a classical building. This was not wholly owing to Pope Sixtus who, as stated, made use of old materials, and the

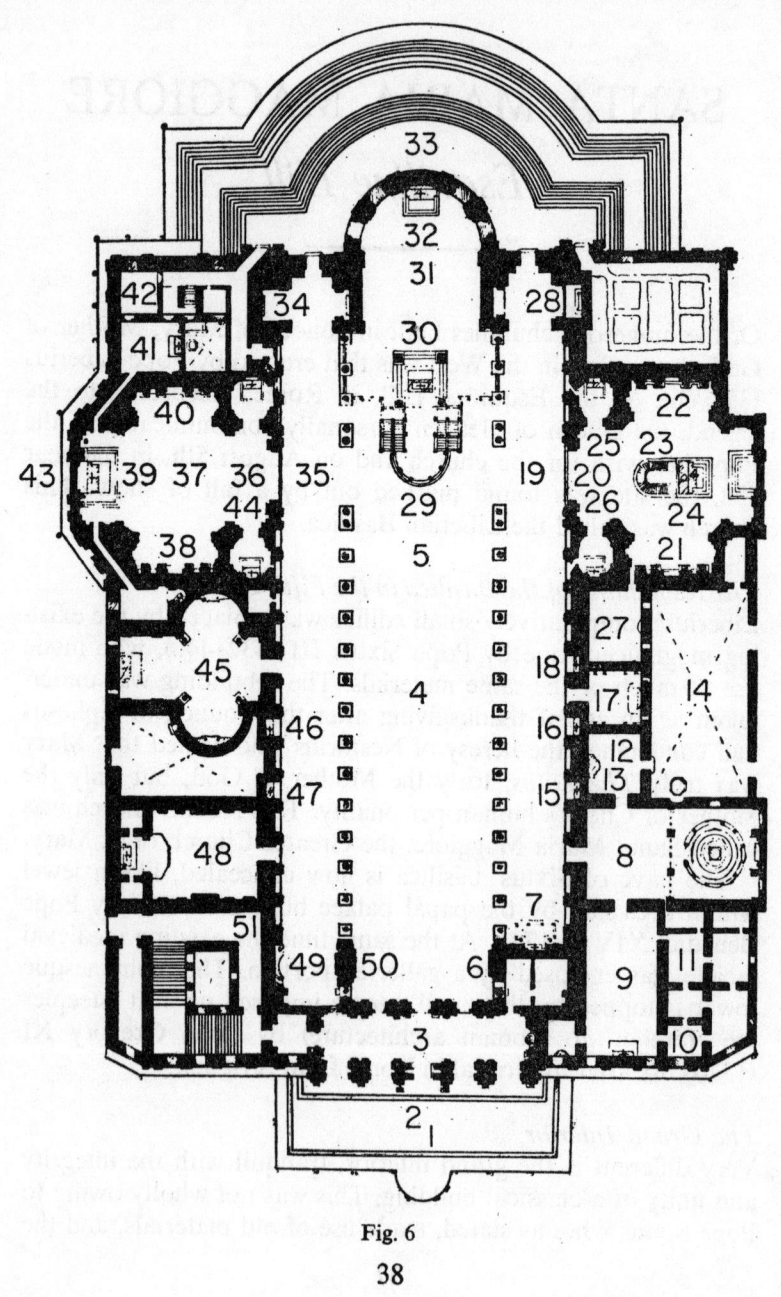

Fig. 6

prevailing unity was established by Benedict XIV's architect, F. Fuga, who reshaped some of the columns and with other ingenious 'tailorings' corrected irregularities.

The chapel on the right-hand side of the nave was built by order of Pope Sixtus V (1585–90). The one on the left-hand side by the Borghese Pope, Paul V, in 1611. Here hangs a famous icon of the Madonna, the *Salus Populi Romani*. From the ceiling of this chapel a shower of white rose petals is caused to flutter down on August 5th each year to commemorate the miraculous fall of snow.

The marble floor of the basilica dates from the twelfth century; the beautiful coffered and gilded ceiling from the fifteenth. This would be unique in Rome but for one in similar style in the church of San Marco.

Mosaics in the Nave and the Triumphal Arch

The supreme adornment is the wonderful series of mosaics of differing periods constituting a wealth of artistic and iconographic interest.

Above the architraves of the nave rectangular panels illustrate events in the lives of Old Testament characters. Nearest to the sanctuary, on one side, Melchidedek offers to God the Father the sacrifice of bread and wine, foreshadowing the Holy

---

Fig. 6

Santa Maria Maggiore
1. The façade—erected 1741, by Ferdinand Fuga.
3. The portico, also the work of Fuga and the same period.
4. The central nave. Above the columns on either side, the series of Old Testament episodes in mosaic.
5. The triumphal arch. Decorated with episodes of the infancy of Christ—under Pope Sixtus III (432–40).
8. The baptistery.
9. The sacristy.
20. Chapel completed under Pope Sixtus V (1585–90).
29. The open confession.
30. High altar.
32. Thirteenth-century mosaics in the apse.
36. Chapel of the Borghese Pope, Paul V, 1611. Contains a famous icon of the Madonna.

Sacrifice of the Mass. This is followed by a three-part tableau where the Eternal appears to Abraham 'seated at the entrance to his tent in the heat of the day' (Gen. xviii). As the Patriarch becomes aware of the Three Mysterious Visitors, he rises to greet them. Then, turning to Sarah he bids her bake three loaves of white flour. Woman-like, Sarah is standing at the door of her abode with an expression of lively curiosity upon her face. Finally the Guests are seated at table, furnished with the three loaves, and Abraham serves with his own hands a lamb, or a kid, upon a dish.

Stylistically, these fascinating panels are reminiscent of illustrations in biblical manuscripts and were possibly copied from one. Their precise date and provenance have caused much learned discussion but they are without question some of the earliest Christian mosaics in existence and could have been taken from Liberius' basilica.

Upon the wide arch that spans the apse episodes from the New Testament treat of the Infancy of Christ. These are of dogmatic interest for they were composed and set up by Pope Sixtus III with intent to emphasize the divine nature *from birth* of the Holy Child, in contradistinction to the declaration of Nestorius that he 'could never believe in a God of a few months old'.

Colourfully presented, these themes are based on pseudo-Matthew rather than upon the canonical gospels. In the episode of the Adoration of the Magi concentration upon the divinity of the Infant-Saviour gave birth to a conception unique in early iconography, for Christ is represented as a child of about two years of age seated alone upon a wide jewelled throne; in his halo is a minute cross. In all other instances, as Babe or as Young Child, he is in the arms or upon the knee of his mother. Mary is seated to one side of the throne, arrayed with the regality of a Byzantine empress. On the other side, a woman clad in a dark mantle holds a scroll half-open upon her knee. The identity of this contemplative, enigmatic figure has never been fully solved. Perhaps the most acceptable of the conjectures is that of Professor Cecchelli who, comparing her to the two women in the mosaic inscription in the church of Santa Sabina, suggests that, while they symbolize the visible Church, she represents the mystical Church which came down to earth, embodying the Divine Wisdom, when the Word became Incarnate. Cecchelli suggests that the half-open scroll may indicate the Book of Seth.[1]

In passing it may be noted that in these mosaics angels have been given wings. This was a novelty in Christian iconography, where angels had been depicted, as in the gospel narratives, as 'men in white garments'.

In the centre of the arch is the solemn and mystical theme of the *Hetimasía*, the Preparation of the Throne for the second coming of Christ. Thus the Advent, when Christ will come as Judge, is united theologically with the Advent when he came as Redeemer.

The Mosaics in the Apse

At the close of the thirteenth century Pope Nicholas IV rebuilt the apse and adorned it with a beautiful mosaic executed by the Franciscan artist, Fra Torriti, who had worked on the mosaic in the Lateran. Here the chosen theme has shifted the emphasis from the child to the mother or, more correctly, to the son's delight to honour her.

In a large central medallion upheld by angels on the wing the two are seated upon a cushioned throne. With his right hand Christ is setting a crown upon Our Lady's head; in his left hand he holds a book open at the words: 'Come My Chosen One and share My throne'.

This theme, the *Coronation of the Virgin*, found here its first expression in a Roman church but was based upon the *Enthronement of Mary* in the century-and-a-half earlier mosaic in the church of Santa Maria in Trastevere.

The figure of Pope Nicholas, wearing the tiara with a single crown, is kneeling at one side of the medallion and Cardinal

[1] C. Cecchelli, *I Mosaici della Basilica di S. Maria Maggiore*, 1956.

Colonna on the other side. Flanking the former are Saints Peter and Paul and St Francis of Assisi, whose tunic is open at the side to disclose his stigmata. St John the Baptist, St John the Evangelist and St Anthony of Padua accompany the Cardinal.

The Relic of the Manger

The devotional treasures of the basilica include the body of St Matthias, beneath the high altar; a blood-stained dalmatic believed to have been worn by St Thomas of Canterbury, and the relic of the Holy Manger. This last had been brought from the Holy Land in the seventh century and consists of but a few rough boards. No documentary proofs of the authenticity of this relic exists, but it is, if no more, an objective symbol of Catholic belief in and Catholic devotion to the stupendous dogma of the Incarnation to which the whole glorious basilica bears witness.

SAN LORENZO IN PANISPERNA
Via Panisperna

In the Via Panisperna, on the right-hand side of the descent from the Piazza Esquilino, is one of the numerous churches dedicated in honour of St Lawrence, Rome's 'third patron saint'. This commemorates the site of his death by burning upon a gridiron and in the eighth century it was listed in the Itinerary of Einsiedeln as *San Lorenzo in Formoso ubi assatus est* (where he was burned).

It was a popular place of pilgrimage and in the eleventh century was spoken of as one of the richest churches in the city.

Rebuilt in the Thirteenth Century
Towards the close of the thirteenth century, the church was rebuilt and reconsecrated by Pope Boniface VIII (1294–1303), and the curious appellation *in Panisperna* came into use. One suggestion refers it to the distribution of bread and ham that was made from the porch in memory of the charities of St Lawrence, the beloved deacon. It is more likely to have been a nickname connected with the district, since the street has the same name.

An attractive entrance up a double stairway gives access to an enclosed forecourt with a short avenue of trees. This small retreat now serves as a cloister for the Franciscan Friars who live in the adjoining house. Before their advent a community of Poor Clares made their home here for some five centuries.

The charm of the approach does not extend to the edifice for the plain rather neglected-looking façade prefaces an interior altered by Cardinal Sirleto in the sixteenth century from its medieval aspect to that of a Baroque-type church.

Six lateral chapels flank the nave. The square sanctuary has a vaulted ceiling. Behind the altar is a large painting of the martyrdom of St Lawrence who from his bed of torment maintains the air of a victor, as indeed he was. It is said to have been the work of a pupil of Michelangelo.

St Bridget of Sweden

The church was a favourite one with St Bridget of Sweden who would sit on the steps collecting alms for the poor pilgrims living in the hospital she had founded. After her death (October 8, 1377), her body was moved, at her own request from the Brigitine Convent in the Piazza Farnese to the house of the Poor Clares and for two days it lay in state in the church. When St Catherine, St Bridget's daughter, returned to Rome it was with their Community she chose to live. Catherine was given the cell her mother had occupied and there St Catherine of Sienna came often to visit her.

Amongst the treasures of San Lorenzo in Panisperna are St Bridget's cloak and office book.

Saints Crispin and Crispinian

Also venerated here are relics of the martyrs Saints Crispin and Crispinian, missionaries who had laboured in Gaul, chiefly in Soissons where they earned their bread, like St Paul, by manual labour, repairing shoes and working in leather. Their names were familiar throughout Europe in the Middle Ages, but in England are chiefly remembered in Shakespeare's lines:

> He that shall live this day, and see old age,
> Will yearly on the vigil feast his neighbours,
> And say, Tomorrow is Saint Crispian;
> Then will he strip his sleeve and show his scars
> And say, These wounds I had on Crispin's day.
> *(Henry V,* Act IV, v. 3)

Today, this somewhat out-of-the-world church has an air of retirement; as of one guarding a past richer in memories than

SAN LORENZO IN PANISPERNA

in present activities. But on its stational day it comes alive and a long procession of clergy and pilgrims leaves the church and wends its way across the courtyard to descend to the crypt beneath the sanctuary, there to venerate a dark rectangular cavity, the Chapel of the Oven, the traditional site of the martyrdom.

SANTI APOSTOLI
Via dei Santi Apostoli

The church of the Holy Apostles occupies one side of an irregular piazza, a few steps away from the Corso, the main thoroughfare that connects the Piazza Venetia with the vast Piazza dell' Popolo. The name Corso derived from the one-time hilarious sport of racing riderless horses from one end to the other of the street where, today, the most skilled horseman could scarcely wend a perilous way.

The once imposing façade of Santi Apostoli has suffered by reason of the risen level of the ground and by the imposition of a Baroque gallery upon its fifteenth-century portico.

This approach effectively disguises an ancient origin, for the foundation goes back to the days of Pope Pelagius I (556-61), and of his successor John III (561-74), whose names were coupled in an inscription in the apse:

> Pelagius coepit, complevit Johannes
> Unum opus amborum par micat et praemium[1]

Byzantine Influence on the Architecture
In the sixth century, Rome was in Byzantine occupation and the church, dedicated in the names of St Philip and St James, was built at the instigation of General Narses; paid for from imperial funds, and constructed by engineers from Ravenna. This Eastern influence explains the plan whereby nave and aisles led into a transept with apsidal ends, thus forming with the semi-circular apse a trefoil choir. At the close of the sixth century Rome offered an immense mine of materials and the

---

[1] Pelagius began, Pope John completed. One their work, one their shining reward.

builders showed no reluctance in adopting them. It is probable that the eight beautiful spirally-grooved marble columns now adorning the Chapel of the Crucifixion at the head of the right-hand aisle came from the Forum of Trajan.

Possession of the bodies of the two Apostles caused the church to rank in prestige with the greater basilicas and many privileges were accorded to it by successive popes.

Rebuilt in the Ninth Century

Pope Adrian I (772–95), added a portico with an atrium but in the ninth century the church began to lose its early splendour, chiefly because of damage by earthquake and by floodings from the Tiber. After the disastrous inundation of 865 Pope Stephen VI (885–91) had to rebuild on a reduced scale. But the Pope loved the church—the parish church of his family—and gave it many gifts: lamps, vases, precious materials; and honoured it with a large number of sacred relics from the catacombs including the bodies of two famous martyrs, Saints Daria and Chrysanthus, who had been buried alive in a sand pit on the Via Salaria.

A Third Phase

A third phase came under Pope Martin V (1417–31), who 'With great care renovated the church of the Twelve Apostles and enlarged the contiguous palace'. There is an interesting medal extant with the bust of Pope Martin V on the obverse and on the reverse the façade of the basilica before it received its Baroque superstructure. No reference to the Twelve Apostles is recorded before the thirteenth century and St Philip and St James remain the titular saints.

The Apostles' Bodies Discovered

In 1701, the whole interior was restyled by Francesco and Carlo Fontana and the ancient granite columns in the nave with their Ionic and Byzantine capitals were swept away. A century and a half later it was decided to reconstruct the confession beneath the high altar. While this work was in progress the bodies of the two Apostles were found enclosed within a sarcophagus-altar of the sixth century that despite the many disasters of the past seems never to have been moved. The shrine stood nearly one and a half metres above the floor-level of the original apse, an arrangement recalling the disposition of Constantine's monument above the tomb of St Peter.

In the eccentric taste of the day the new confession was formed to resemble a catacomb gallery with *loculi* (wall graves) inscriptions, and mural paintings, an arrangement described by Professor Marrucchi as a solecism in archaeology because catacombs were never constructed within the walls of a city.

From the centre of the sanctuary a stair descends to this unusual crypt where a modern sarcophagus containing the sacred remains of St Philip and St James stands beneath an altar.

ST PETER'S BASILICA
Piazza di San Pietro

Familiar to every pilgrim, as indeed to the stay-at-home Christian, is the exterior of the vast building, a blend of the Renaissance style with that of the Baroque, which commemorates the burial-place of St Peter, and whose dome dominates the Roman skyline; the dome that enshrines six feet of earth and nineteen centuries of history.

The basilica stands above its predecessor, Old St Peter's, of which the remarkable construction has been revealed during the modern explorations of the foundations. As these discoveries have now been recorded in numerous books and journals a brief historical summary is all that is called for here.

In antiquity it was illegal to construct tombs within the walls of a city and many of the roads that stretched out across the Roman campagna were bordered with *columbaria* (crypts with niches for urns, like dovecotes) and by the imposing *mausolea* of patrician families. Of these, the rotunda now called Castel Sant' Angelo, built in A.D. 130 by the Emperor Hadrian, is the best existing example.

After St Peter had been condemned to death he was led out, according to tradition, across the Tiber to the Vatican Valley, at the foot of the Vatican Hill, where the circus of Caligula and Nero had been newly erected. There he was crucified, head downwards. To the south of the circus ran a road where a few unpretentious tombs had been made. Amongst these in an unappropriated plot, or one that belonged to a Christian, the Apostle's body was laid in a surface grave, now known to have been a very humble one, for the Christians like the Jews rejected the more popular fashion of cremation.

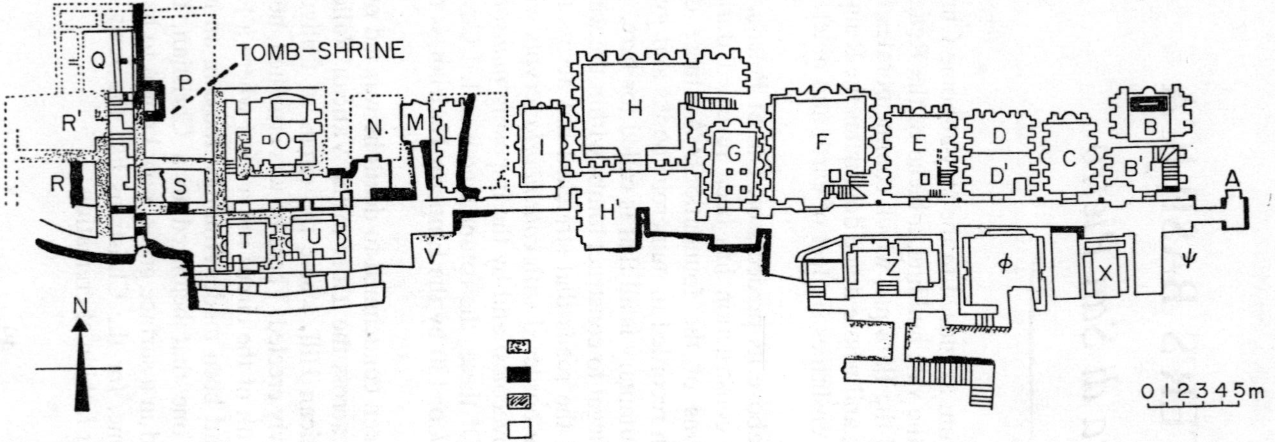

Fig. 7

The street of the pagan sepulchres over which Constantine raised his memorial church to St. Peter. The letters indicate the family or collegiate chambers. P is the small court that fronted the Apostle's shrine. M is a tiny chamber made for a pagan child but afterwards used for the tomb of a Christian and on the ceiling is a mosaic of *Christus-Helios*. 'In the centre of the vault the theme of triumph over death reaches its climax in the figure of the risen and ascending Christ, the new *Sol Invictus Christus-Helios*, radiant with Easter light' (*The Shrine of St Peter*, Toynbee and Perkins). Z was the chamber of the Egyptians. A (last in the line) has a *titulus* (name plate) over the entrance. This was the property of Gaius Popilius Heracla, a 'circus fan' who desired to be buried *in Vatic(ano) ad circum*, i.e. close to the Vatican Circus.

The Memorial Above the Grave

Above this grave a small memorial, alcove-like in form, was presently erected. A trustworthy reference to this exists in the correspondence, about the year 200, between a Christian priest named Gaius and a Montanist schismatic called Proclus: 'I can show you,' wrote Gaius, 'the trophies [i.e. the martyr-shrines] of the Apostles. For if you go to the Vatican or to the Ostian Way there you will find the trophies of those who founded the Church.' (Eusebius, H.E. ii, 25.6.77.) St Paul had been buried on the road to Ostia.

Until the bitter persecution of the Christians under Valerian in 258 pilgrims frequently went to pray at the Apostles' graves for a strict law protected all places of sepulchre. During the persecution it was forbidden, under penalty of death, to enter the cemeteries, but graves do not seem to have been desecrated and when Constantine the Great came to build his memorial church in the early fourth century: 'He had no need to seek out the tomb of St Peter, this was in his time present to the eyes of all and the object of flourishing devotion.'[1]

Constantine's Basilica

The popularity of the Vatican region for burials had by the early fourth century greatly increased. A double line of closely-set tombs, many of them elaborately decorated, stretched along the foot of the hill. Although occasionally a Christian had his sarcophagus, or *loculus* (a wall-tomb), in one of these chambers, none had been made for Christians. The one small room which has Christian mosaics on the vault and on the walls had been originally the place of burial of a young pagan child. It must then have been to the scandalized amazement of the majority of his subjects that the Emperor Constantine chose this popular sepulchral area, still in regular use, in which to build a church. Modern society, afflicted with the unpredictable plans

[1] *Esplorazioni sotto la confessione di San Pietro in Vaticano esequiti negli anni 1940–1949.*

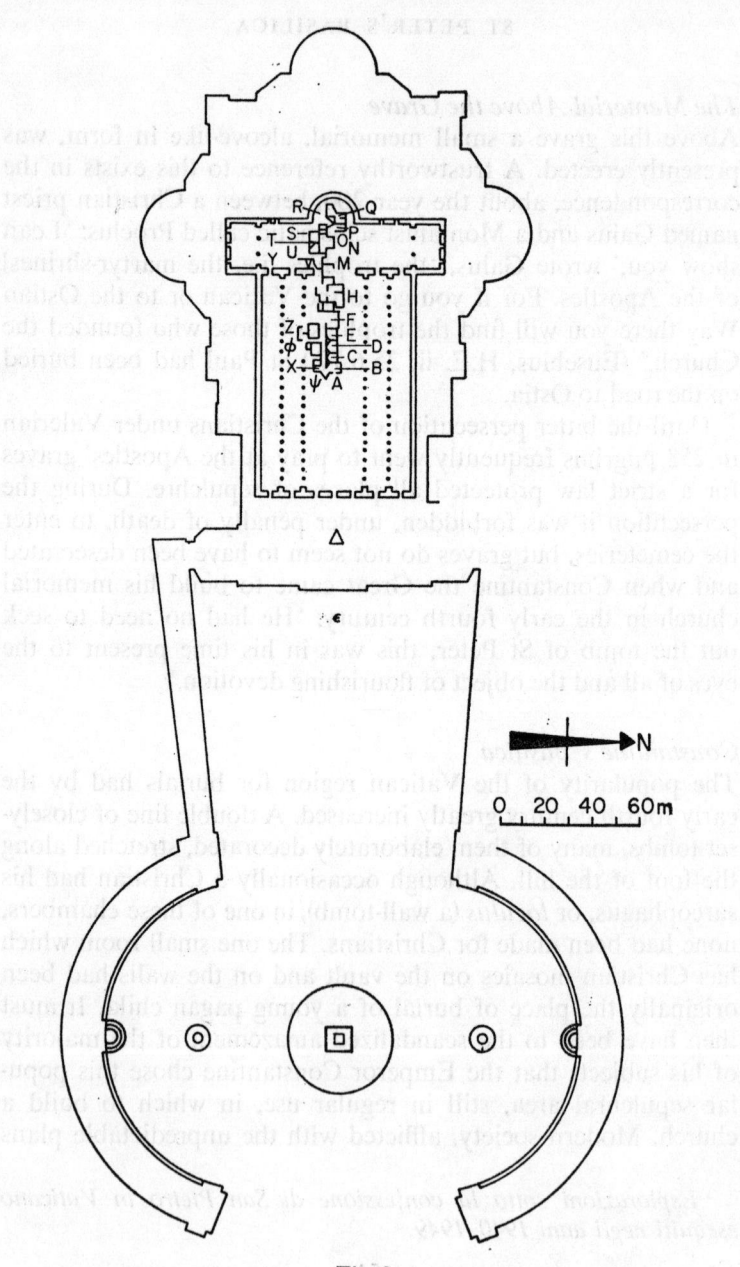

Fig. 8

of the 'developers', could sympathize with the consternation of the Romans at such a decision.

And a remarkable one it was, for not only were religious and legal problems involved, but the physical difficulties of the site might reasonably have been thought overwhelming.

'In order to make a level terrace on which to build his church, Constantine's engineers had to cut back the steep southeastern slope of the Vatican Hill and to build out from it an enormous platform, an operation which involved the cutting and dumping of over a million cubic feet of earth... within this area those tombs that stood in the way of the great longitudinal foundations of the nave of Constantine's church were ruthlessly demolished and their remains packed with earth, their superstructure dismantled and the gaps between them linked with strengthening walls... this was drastic action and the Emperor even if not technically guilty of *violatio sepulchri* could not have escaped the odium of putting out of action an extensive area of well-cared-for family sepulchres.'[1]

Why Constantine chose the basilican form for his churches (and whence that form derived) has been much debated, but that it was one eminently suited, with regional divergence, to the liturgical requirements is indisputable. In the slightly earlier church of the Lateran, where no martyr's grave had to be considered, the plan could be followed without complications. Here the matter was different, and a transept was inserted separating the body of the church from the area of the shrine, which as the focal point of the whole building was left to stand above the level of the floor.

[1] Jocelyn Toynbee and J. Ward Perkins, *The Shrine of St Peter*, 1956.

Fig. 8

Outline plan of the existing basilica surrounding Constantine's basilica which he raised above the street of pagan tomb-chambers. The letters indicate these chambers (see fig. 7).

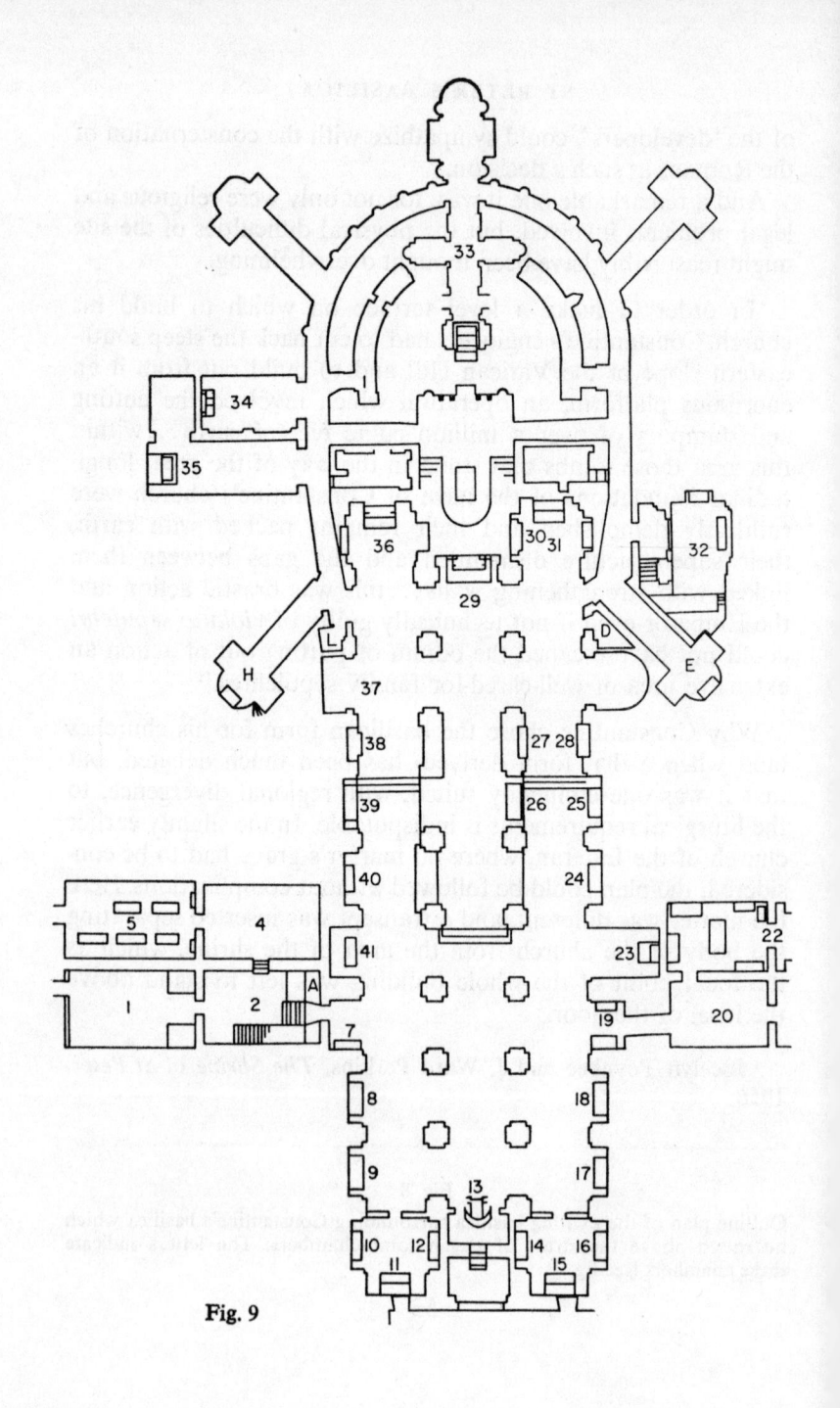

Fig. 9

The Appearance of the Shrine

The marble casing had an opening towards the nave permitting pilgrims to thrust their heads and shoulders within it, and to let down pieces of cloth to gain contact with the tomb, to be carried away as precious relics.

One of the surprises for the modern excavators was to find that the altar had not at first been set above the shrine, but somewhere in front of it. When St Jerome wrote (in his exposition *Contra Vivilantium*) 'Is it an evil thing that the bishop does when he sacrifices to God over what are to us the hallowed bones, to you the miserable dust, of dead men, Peter and Paul, and when he treats their tombs as the altars of Christ', it must have been within the precincts of the sanctuary.

Under Pope Gregory the Great (590–604) considerable changes were carried out around the shrine and as these made it impossible for pilgrims to approach in the old way, Gregory opened up a semi-circular crypt from the centre of which a short gallery gave access to the rear of the shrine. On account of the depth of this gallery it came very close to the underlying grave.

During these alterations the beautiful spiral marble columns imported by Constantine from the Orient to support a canopy over the shrine were moved and set in a line in front of the sanctuary.

Fig. 9

Plan of the crypt beneath St Peter's which has been reconstructed to form a secondary basilica with its own exterior entrance. This opens to the south 'aisle' through chambers where fragments of sculpture and sarcophagi are preserved. The aisle is entered from Chamber 2 which also has a second stairway that descends to the street of the pagan sepulchres. Some twenty popes (including the only English pope, Adrian IV), one emperor and two queens have their tombs in the crypt; the numerals aligning the walls mark the positions. At the sanctuary end, the semi-circular gallery opens to two chapels. No. 33 is the Clementine Chapel behind whose altar was discovered part of the shrine set by Constantine above the Apostle's grave, lying five feet beneath. The chapel on the opposite side contains the tomb of Pope Pius XII. That of his successor Pope John XXIII, is not far away, in the north aisle.

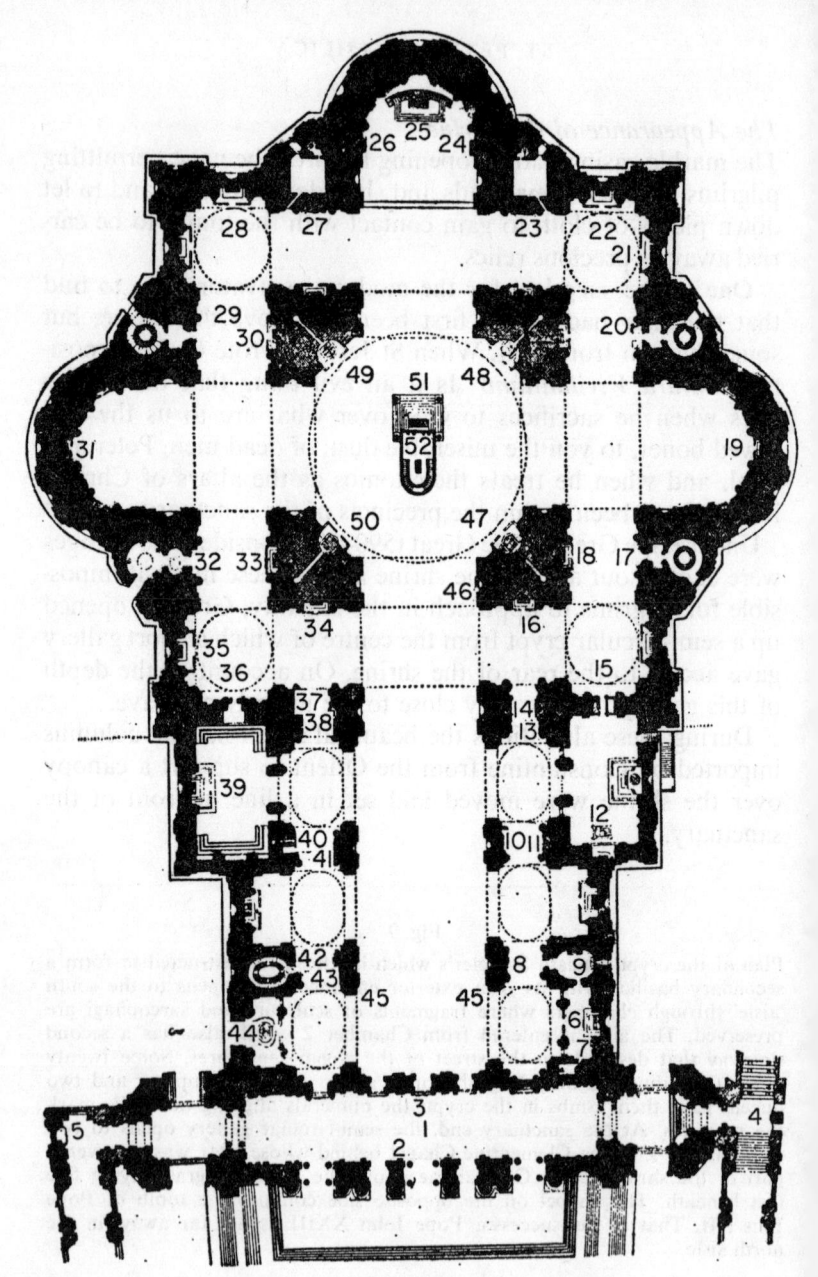

Fig. 10

ST PETER'S BASILICA

The Basilica Rebuilt in the Sixteenth Century
For nearly twelve hundred years the basilica remained in use, although in increasing danger of collapse. After several false starts, rebuilding began in earnest in 1505. Demolition began at the sanctuary-end and to protect the high altar and the tomb beneath it the Renaissance architect, Bramante, enclosed the area in a species of classical temple that remained *in situ* until the close of the century. When Michelangelo was in charge of the work, he raised a wall across the nave so that services could continue at the atrium end.

In 1625, the immense building reached its final stage. Then a problem arose that exercised architectural resource: how to cover the altar with a canopy sufficiently imposing to counteract the dwarfing effect to the stupendous dome.

Bernini's Bronze Canopy
The problem devolved finally upon Bernini, who designed a

Fig. 10

St Peter's
1. Vestibule, by Carlo Maderno.
2. Giotto's mosaic of the *navicella* (ship symbol of the Church).
4. Statue of Constantine the Great.
5. Statue of Charlemagne.
6. Michelangelo's famous *Pietà*.
12. Chapel of the Blessed Sacrament.
25. Bernini's bronze monument enshrining the ancient *cathedra* (bishop's throne).
31. Guido Reni's crucifixion of St Peter.
39. Canons' choir.
43. Canova's tomb of the Stuarts.
44. Baptistery. The porphyry lid of the Emperor Hadrian's sarcophagus used for the font.
46. Seated statue of St Peter.
47. Statue of Longinus, holding his spear.
48. Statue of St Helena, holding the Cross.
49. Statue of Veronica, holding the veil.
50. Statue of St Andrew.
51. Bernini's canopy over the high altar.
52. The open confession (space in front of the altar) with Canova's kneeling statue of Pope Pius VI.

bronze baldachin supported on bronze columns ninety feet high, and so overcame the difficulty of diffusing the light.

With its columns twisted like giant sticks of barley sugar this masterpiece is more often an object of astonishment than of admiration, but its interest is heightened when it is recalled that Bernini copied his columns from Constantine's marble ones. Happily, he did not discard the beautiful marbles, but set them in reliquary recesses made in the four great pilasters of the dome to house the major relics of the basilica: the Veil of Veronica; the Spear of Longinus; a portion of the True Cross and the skull of St Andrew. Until 1462 the Apostle's skull had been preserved in Patras, but was sent to Rome for safe keeping when Turkish invasion was threatened. In 1964, it was returned to the Greek Orthodox Church.

The Niche of the Pallia
When the pilgrim enters the basilica (feeling of pigmy stature as he glances at the six-feet-high cherubs who offer him holy water from their giant shells), he naturally goes first to the high altar, there to kneel at the rail of the Open Confession. Beneath a row of lamps, he sees two bronze doors. Enclosed behind them is a recess approximately eight feet by four. In this recess, called the Niche of the Pallia, the woollen vestments (*pallia*) are enclosed before the pope sends them to the archbishops. The *pallium*, worn also by the pope, is symbolic of pastoral charge in guiding and guarding Christ's flock. The reason for placing them in the Niche is that it is situated immediately above the grave of St Peter to whom the Lord gave the injunction: 'Feed My lambs; feed My sheep'.

The Finding of St Peter's Grave
Close behind the Niche of the Pallia is a tiny chapel (the Cappella Clementina) formed by Pope Clement VIII (1592–1605) within the gallery that gave access to the rear of the shrine. In the recent search for the grave the altar in the chapel was taken down and behind it were found a medieval altar and the upper part of the marble casing placed around the shrine

by Constantine. Five feet lower in the ground, lying at an oblique angle, was the earthen grave.

The Street of Pagan Sepulchres

At the rebuilding in the sixteenth century the old basilica became the crypt of its successor, with the sarcophagi of many of the popes lining its walls. This has been completely reorganized and made into a secondary basilica with its own exterior entrance that opens into a series of chambers. From the third of these rooms an iron stair descends to the Street of the Pagan Sepulchres giving access to those now cleared of the rubble with which Constantine's engineers had packed them. In this fascinating City of the Dead lingers the spirit of the twilight era when myths of paganism were dying and the dawn of Christian truth slowly breaking.

So stands St Peter's vast memorial, embodying Christian history since Christ.

SANTA MARIA IN DOMNICA
Caelian Hill

This charming church takes the pilgrim topographically to the crown of the Caelian Hill; historically to a memorial of one of the great events in the life of the Catholic Church, the Iconoclastic controversy, which had repercussions of political as well as of ecclesiastical importance.

From the days of Pope Gregory II (715–31), the papacy maintained for more than a century a struggle against the iconoclastic emperors of Byzantium, and until the final victory the fate of art in Europe hung in the balance.

'We might have had churches decorated with arabesques and inscriptions, as in the mosques, but we should not have had the grand tympana of the Romanesque churches, the thousand statues of the cathedrals, the frescoes of Giotto nor those of Fra Angelico... the popes were capable of replying to the arguments of the innovators who showed the dangers of a return to paganism... but the popes showed themselves as intelligent as they were courageous: they did not desire to mutilate the human spirit and they saved art. They acted in the eighth and ninth centuries as in the sixteenth when the Protestants burnt the pictures and destroyed the statues: they defended civilization.'[1]

Diaconal Churches
Towards the close of the struggle the diaconal church of Santa Maria in Domnica was built by Pope Paschal I (817–24), and the existing building is substantially his. The title 'in Domnica' does not imply, as is sometimes stated, derivation from a

[1] E. Mâle, *Rome et ses vieilles églises*, p. 101.

dominicum (domestic chapel) for such had not been established here. Of the suggestions put forward one is that it derived from *dominica sotto praedia*, i.e. that the church was sited in an area of imperial dependence. Excavations beneath the foundations have revealed the existence of a public building thought to have been a barrack of the *Vigiles* (fire brigade?). Within this building a Christian oratory had been built in the sixth or seventh century, connected with a diaconal hall. Owing to the failure of the civic powers to make the customary distributions of food, especially of corn, in times of scarcity, this duty had to be taken over by the Church and by the close of the eighth century no less than eighteen diaconal centres existed in Rome. The greater number bore the title 'Santa Maria', followed by an indication of the locality.

Architectural Features and Decoration
The exterior of Paschal's church probably conformed to the normal paleo-Christian basilica. The actual façade and its portico are the work of Cardinal de' Medici, later Pope Leo X (1513–21). The architect was Andrea da Monte San Savino, commonly called Sansovino, who in compliment to Pope Leo set a lion's mask into the key-stone of each of the arches of the portico.

The spacious nave retains its classic form. Many of the columns are of granite with capitals of varying Corinthian character. These form an amusing study, conveniently arranged.

The walls above the arcading were refashioned and painted in the early sixteenth century. The slightly later coffered ceiling is a splendid example of its kind. This was a gift of Cardinal Ferdinando Medici and his coat-of-arms occupies the central panel. The small compartments have reliefs that illustrate with symbolic attributes the Litany of Mary; the star; ark; vase; throne; temple, etc.

Pope Paschal's Apsidal Mosaic
The dominating feature, however, is the mosaic composition with which Pope Paschal I covered the apse and its arch. He

was a devoted venerator of the saints and in the three churches connected with his name he made plain his love for sacred images. That he was susceptible to Eastern influence in art is exemplified here as in his mosaics in the church of Santa Prassede, where his artists were refugees from Byzantium for whom he provided material as well as spiritual support.

At the summit of the arch Christ is seated upon a rainbow. The rainbow-throne was an artifice used in the Orient to express pictorially the verses of Ezechiel in which the Prophet compares to the rainbow the Light shining from the Eternal. Two angels and the twelve Apostles accompany Christ. St Peter holds his keys, an attribute never omitted by Pope Paschal, perhaps not without political nuance since it was in his papacy that spiritual prerogatives between pope and emperor were more clearly defined, and a pope could be elected without first obtaining the imperial consent.

The theme in the apse was one new to Rome in that position in a church. Seated upon a jewelled throne, the Madonna holds the Child in full frontal posture. A pose of hieratic dignity which centuries later inspired the monumental sculpture in the tympanum of the west door of Chartres cathedral.

In the mosaic, this central group is surrounded by a close-pressed throng of angels in white robes with wings of gold, their blue, commingling haloes giving the impression of a countless array. At the foot of the throne Pope Paschal is kneeling, his whole attitude eloquent of his desire to exalt and honour the Mother and the Child whose images were being insulted and destroyed by the iconoclasts. Well could he quote the words of the psalmist: 'I have loved the beauty of thy house and the place where thy glory dwelleth.'

The confession beneath the altar is modern (1958), but some valuable fragments from the medieval choir enclosure have been inserted in the walls.

Standing in the sunshine of a Roman morning, looking back from the portico, the pilgrim can take pleasure in the knowledge that this gracious fane is again the centre of parochial life as the outcrop of the modern city rises around it.

SAN CLEMENTE
Piazza di San Clemente

The basilica of St Clement is not only one of exceptional attraction to the ordinary visitor but also one that raises intriguing problems for the archaeologist and the historian of art.

There was more than one Clement to whom the first-century tenement whose lower rooms were incorporated into the church could have belonged. What seems assured is that it had been in the possession of a Roman patrician of that name and that a Christian meeting-place had existed within it at an early date. The Christian community acquired this property, by bequest or by purchase, and altered it in such a manner that while the exterior retained its customary aspect, the interior contained rooms adapted for communal worship. It was listed amongst the Christian properties sequestered by the pagan government in the third century, but was afterwards restored to the Church.

A formal basilica was erected on the site by Pope Siricius (384-99), who dedicated it under the invocation of St Clement of Rome, the third successor to the See of St Peter, as recorded in Siricius' inscription.

In 417 Pope Zosimus, who was much troubled by the Pelagian heresy (Pelagius denied the necessity of sanctifying grace), held a council in the new church and concerning this matter he wrote to St Augustine: 'We sat in the basilica of St Clement, for he, imbued with the teaching of blessed Peter the Apostle, had corrected the ancient errors with authority.'

The Basilica Rebuilt in the Twelfth Century
Pope Siricius' church remained in use until its partial destruction when Robert Guiscard's soldiery set fire to this part of the city, while attempting the rescue of the beleaguered Pope

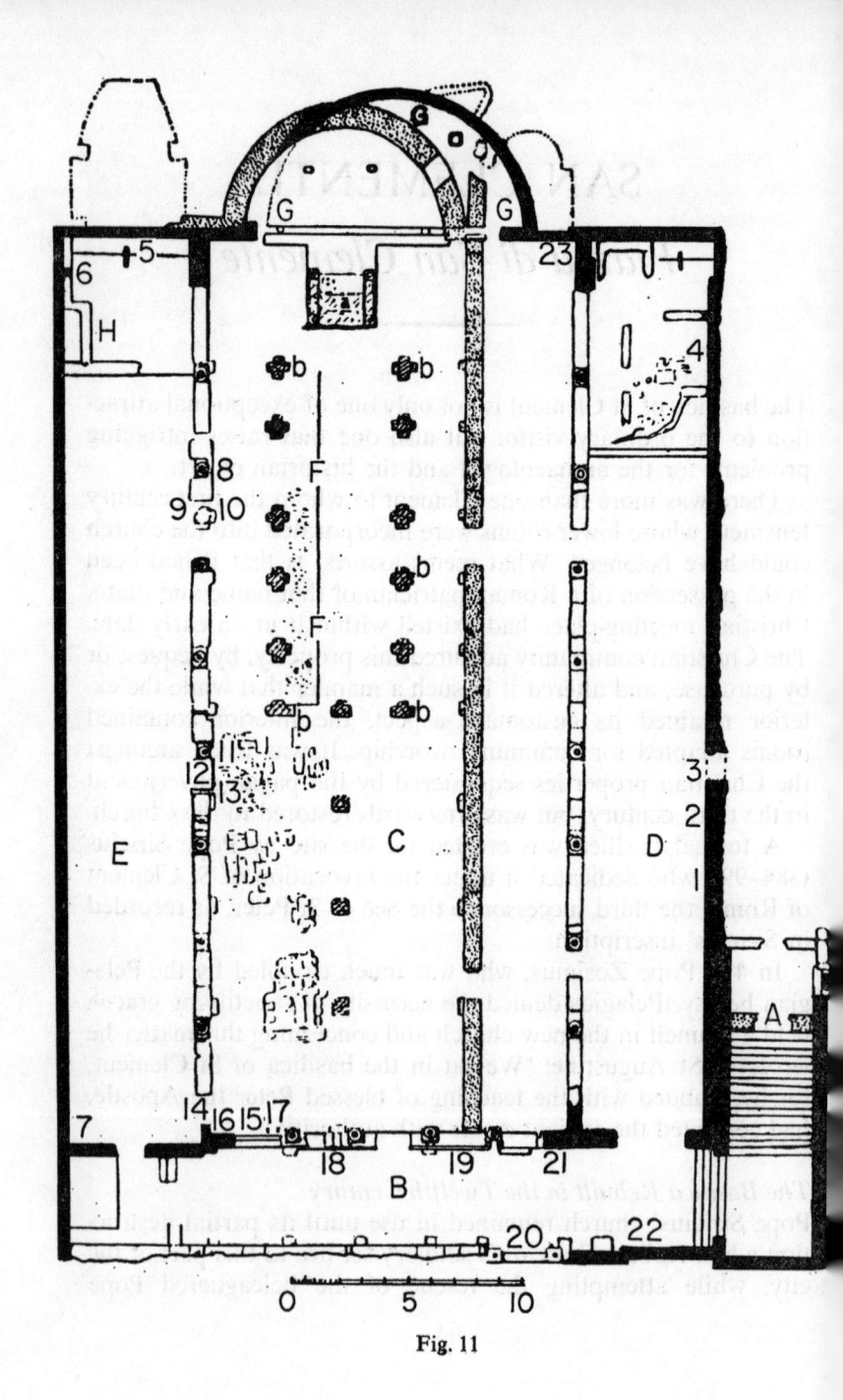

Fig. 11

Gregory VII (1073–85). Efforts to restore it proved unsatisfactory and the shell was filled in with the rubble and a new building raised above it. This followed the same plan, even to the inclusion of a porticoed atrium, a feature that had become exceptional by that time. In the earlier centuries these charming forecourts had served a liturgical purpose. In the centre stood a fountain into which fingers were dipped in ritual cleansing as into the small holy-water stoops in church porches today. In the shelter of the portico the catechumens received instruction and penitents knelt in public view, begging intercessory prayers from their more fortunate brethren passing into the church for Mass. (No mere 'Three Hail Marys' in those days!)

Discovery of the First Basilica and its Frescoes

As the centuries passed, the fact that the church of San Clemente had been rebuilt was forgotten and the existing edifice came to be regarded as the original one. It was only in the nineteenth century that doubts about its origin led the Irish Dominican Prior, Father Mullooly, to begin the investigations that revealed the truth. Explorations carried out over a long period have brought to light the existence of three superimposed structures. Of these the lowest, now some forty feet below the level of the modern street, constituted the ground floor of the house of Clement.

One of the surprises for the excavators was to find the walls in the nave and those in the narthex of the earlier church

---

Fig. 11
San Clemente
Lower basilica.
A.   Entrance.
B.   Narthex, with medieval frescoes.
C.   Central nave—frescoes on the inners walls indicated by the numbers.
D.   Right-hand aisle, with frescoes 1, 2, 3 and 4. No. 2 an important niche with Madonna and Child.
E.   Left-hand aisle. No. 6 fresco of a bishop baptizing.
G.1. Black line indicates original apse.
G.2. Smaller apse—constructed in the twelfth century to support the upper church.

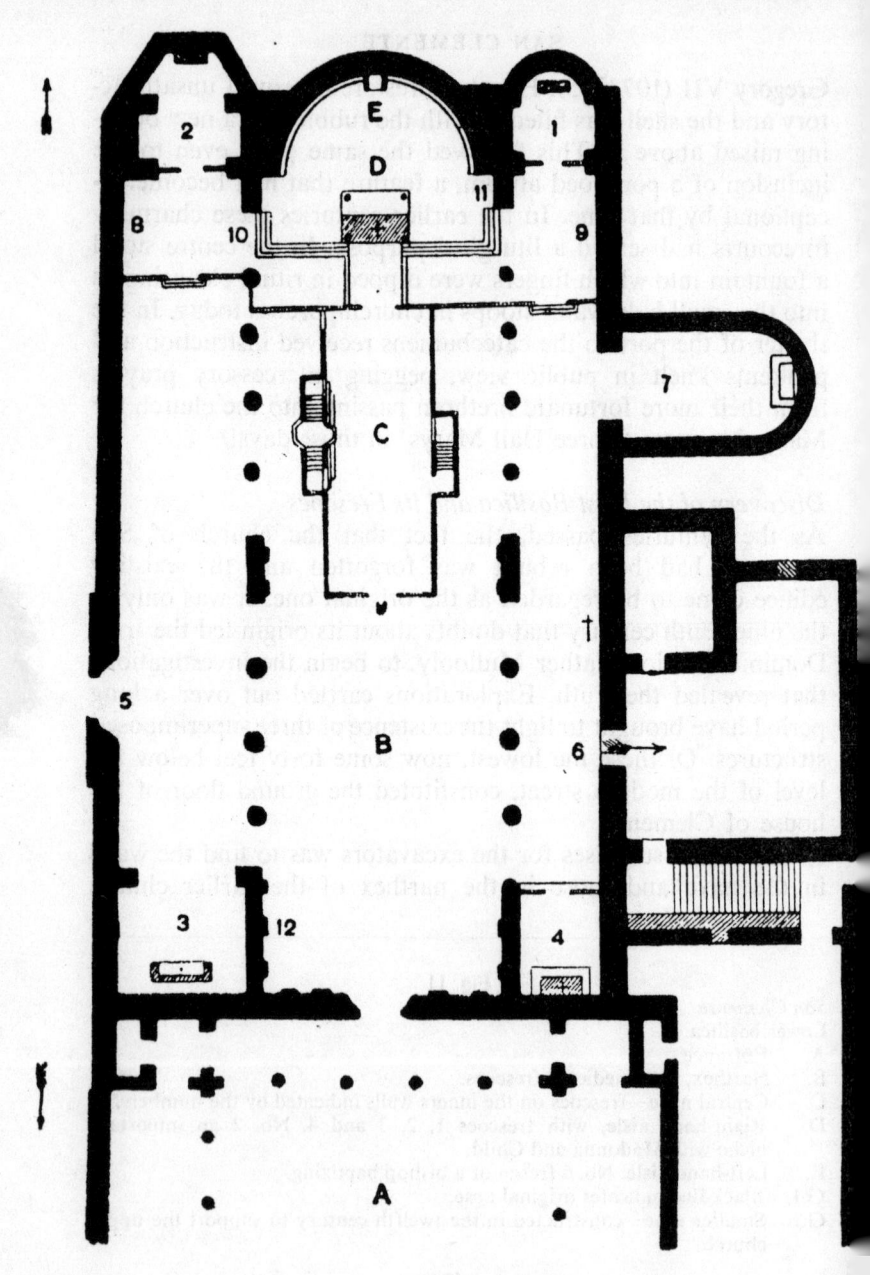

Fig. 12

Santa Maria in Domnica
Pope Paschal I's ninth-century mosaic in the apse. The coffered ceiling, sixteenth century, illustrates symbolism used in the Litany of Mary.

Santa Maria in Domnica
Detail of Pope Paschal's mosaic. Wearing the rectangular halo, he is kneeling at the Madonna's feet.

San Clemente

Built circa 1100, complete wi[th]
porched atrium and propyl[aeum]
(entrance porch). Stands abo[ve]
its fourth-century predecesso[r]
a great deal of which s[till]
exists.

San Clemente

A fresco on a wall in the und[er]
ground church. An Ascensi[on]
of Christ or the Assumption [of]
the Virgin? The vested figu[re]
is Pope Leo III (795-81[6])
wearing the rectangular ha[lo]
who either ordered the pai[nt]
ing or had an earlier subj[ect]
over-painted. The other fron[tal]
figure is that of St Vitus.

painted with frescoes still in comparatively good condition. The period covered stretched from the sixth to the eleventh century, providing a valuable contribution to the history of art in Rome. Those in the narthex, completed shortly before the fire, are votive paintings of delightfully mythical episodes in the life and death of Pope St Clement.

One fresco in the church, probably of the ninth century, is claimed by the Dominican custodians to represent an Assumption of the Virgin into heaven; but it is more probably an Ascension of Christ according to the Syrian formula. There are questionable features for either conjecture and it is not impossible that an Ascension had been overpainted in the time of Pope Leo III (795–816), who felt a particular devotion to the Feast of the Assumption.[1] This possibility recalls a more recent discussion (in 1955), concerning a Byzantine-style Madonna in San Clemente that had been painted, a critic suggested, upon a sixth-century portrait of the Empress Theodora.

The Upper Basilica—Points of Interest
Upon entering San Clemente a momentary disappointment may be felt upon viewing the Renaissance treatment of the walls of the nave, and the stuccoed arches above the ancient columns.

[1] Mgr J. Wilpert.

Fig. 12

San Clemente
Upper basilica—early twelfth century.
A. Atrium with central fountain.
B. Refashioned in eighteenth century.
C. Twelfth-century choir enclosure with side pulpits and Paschal candlestick.
D. High altar with gothic canopy.
E. Bishop's throne with Cardinal Anastasius' inscription.
2. Blessed Sacrament Chapel.
3. Chapel of St Catherine of Alexandria. Important fifteenth-century frescoes.
5. Entrance to the church, from Via S. Giovanni in Laterano.
6. The sacristy.
7. Nineteenth-century chapel of Saints Cyril and Methodius.

But this is quickly dispelled for the church is unique in possessing its full complement of medieval marble furnishings together with one of the more exquisite of the 'Cosmati' pavements.

At the head of the nave is the choir enclosure with its Paschal candlestick and gospel and epistle *ambones* (pulpits). On the epistle (right-hand) side is also a sixth-century marble book-rest used for the reading of the Prophecies in Lent. This had been salvaged from the underlying church together with marble slabs inscribed with Christian symbols and panels bearing the monogram of Pope John II (533–35). These last have been inserted into the sanctuary rails.

The baldachin above the altar has retained the chain from which was suspended the dove-shape ciborium for the Reserved Host, a customary feature before the introduction of a separate tabernacle. (In Tewkesbury Abbey may be seen the effigy of Sir Edward le Despenser, kneeling upon the roof of his chantry chapel facing the sanctuary at the level at which the Dove Ciborium would have been hanging, where he has kept vigil for six hundred years.)

The anchor carved on the pediment of the baldachin makes reference to the (legendary) martyrdom of St Clement who was said to have been cast into the sea with an anchor tied to his neck. A relic of St Ignatius of Antioch, who (certainly) was devoured by wild beasts in the Colosseum, is preserved in the altar stone.

The *cathedra* (episcopal throne) had also been saved after the fire and as the back was broken it was replaced with a piece of marble from a tomb, which explains the word MART incised upon it.[1] An inscription along the border runs: 'Anastasius cardinal-priest of this title began and completed this work.' The work means the rebuilding of the basilica and as the Cardinal died in 1135 the date is exceptionally well known.

Within the semi-dome of the apse shines one of the most beautiful mosaics in Rome. Upon the tall central cross the

[1] It has been suggested to the writer that the part of the throne incised MART could have belonged to the original dedicatory inscription of Pope Siricius (384–97).

Crucified is companioned by twelve white doves symbolizing the Apostles sharing in the Passion of their Lord. Upon the gold and azure background the acanthus spirals hold within their volutes human figures; beasts; birds; all creation redeemed by Christ.

The Chapel of St Catherine of Alexandria

The chapel of St Catherine of Alexandria, at the end of the left-hand aisle, is adorned with frescoes attributed, but controversially, to Massaccio. Episodes from the saint's life cover the side walls. On the main wall is a Crucifixion where Mary is depicted fainting in the arms of the attendant women. This was a novelty which was beginning to come into fashion and culminated in a petition to Pope Julius II (1503–13), to institute a feast in honour of 'Our Lady of the Swoon'. The petition was refused, and the exponents reproved for over-emphasizing human weakness in the Mother of God who could endure suffering without faltering and who *stood* by her Son's cross, as recorded in the gospel narrative, and as represented in all early Christian art.

When this famous painting was detached from the wall in an attempt to arrest the dampness that is defacing it, the artist's cartoon was found beneath it.

The Chapel of SS. Cyril and Methodius

In the right-hand aisle is the chapel of SS. Cyril and Methodius whose missionary labours amongst the Slavonic peoples included the translation of the gospels into their native tongue. St Cyril died in Rome in 869 and was buried in San Clemente. St Methodius became bishop of Sirmium and the place of his burial is uncertain. It was owing to the intercession of these missionaries that Pope Adrian II (867–72) permitted Slavonic converts to use the vernacular in the sacred liturgy and visiting Slavonic priests have always been permitted to use their Rite when celebrating Mass in this church. St Cyril and St Methodius were regarded as the patrons of unity of the Eastern and the Western Churches and it is interesing to recall that it was to their chapel here that Pope John XXIII (1958–63) paid one of his first visits after his enthronement.

The Mithraic Temple

Amongst the many attractions that bring visitors to San Clemente is the existence of the famous Temple of Mithras that is embowelled in the subterranean regions. This dates from the third century. The worship of Mithras was an Oriental mystery cult much in vogue in the Roman army at that time. Its discipline included a form of baptism and esoteric regeneration. The temple is entered by a stair from the lower church.

SANTA BALBINA
Via Antoniniana

This architecturally unusual church is first mentioned in the time of Pope Gregory the Great (590–604), but the masonry and details of construction indicate a much earlier foundation. Whether it was originally built as a Christian edifice, or whether adapted from a pagan one (not a temple) is uncertain.

The form is that of a large hall ending in an apse with a niche for the *cathedra*. Six recesses, alternately apsidal and rectangular, on either side of the nave take the place of aisles. This gives a sense of spaciousness that is increased by the open timber roof.

Situated on the Lower Aventine, St Balbina's stands upon ground rich in ancient Roman remains. Amongst the monuments was the *Templum Bonae Deae Ordatae*, the sanctuary of a goddess who attended to maladies of the eyes and *ex-votos* in the shape of human eyes have been found in the vicinity.

The Emperor Hadrian, who disliked urban Rome, had a house here, but it is doubtful if he visited it very often. Another house belonged to Fabius Cilo, consul in 193 and tutor to the young Caracalla. The latter when Emperor built the public baths the stupendous ruins of which now form the principal landmark of the region. This colossal establishment, from which many famous works of art have been retrieved, covered a vast area and embraced within its perimeter temples, libraries, restaurants and gymnasia.

The Contrasting Fate of the Christian Church
In contrast to the fate of these pretentious monuments, the unobtrusive church has weathered the vicissitudes of the centuries comparatively unharmed. Its plain façade faced by a plain

portico opens to a verdant and peaceful piazza. This accords with a sense of remoteness from the pressure of the world which is well suited to the aged folk, men and women who dwell in the adjoining hospice of Santa Margharita and worship here.

When Professor Muñoz restored the interior in 1928 his adjustments consisted chiefly in the removal of out-of-character accretions; reopening the windows in the nave and the apse and in lowering the floor to its original level. Inset into the pavement that leads from the main door to the choir enclosure (modern) are panels of black and white mosaic that were dug up in recent years and are said to have come from a necropolis of the first century.

Points of Interest
In the third recess on the left-hand side a pleasing medieval fresco of the Madonna and Child enthroned between St Peter and St Paul faces on the opposite wall a Crucifixion finely executed in relief. This was originally in Old St Peter's and is reputed to be a work of Mino da Fiesole. The altar is of Sicilian jasper resplendent in a semi-rococo style. Beneath it in a handsome urn are the bodies of Santa Balbina and of her father, St Quirinus, a tribune under the Emperor Hadrian. Little is known today of Balbina's history beyond the fact that she was esteemed in Rome as a martyr and a catacomb situated between the Via Appia and the Via Ardeatina bears her name.

Although Hadrian was opposed, in principle, to unnecessary bloodshed he disliked the 'sect' of the Christians as he also despised the Jews 'for their ridiculous obsession with their god'. The connexion between this remarkable man and the Christian girl is not without poignancy. While his weary body was lain in the seemingly impregnable security of his vast rotunda on the banks of the Tiber[1] (now known as the Castel Sant' Angelo) and that of the virgin-martyr in an obscure catacomb-grave, *his* soul went forth in anxious quest:

[1] The inverted cover of the porphyry sarcophagus believed to have been Hadrian's now serves as the baptismal font in St Peter's Basilica.

SANTA BALBINA

Animula, vagula, blandula,
Hospes comesque corporis
Quae nunc abibis in loca
Pallidula, rigida, nudula,
Nes, ut soles, dabis iocos.[1]
(P. Aelius Hadrianus, Imp. (to his soul))

while *her* soul departed into the assurance of the resurrection in Christ:

Balbina, vivas in Domino[2]

[1] 'Little wandering soul of mine guest and comrade of my body. where are you off to now? Little pale stiff and naked one—no more joking for you.' (Literal translation, by J. M. C. Toynbee.)
[2] 'Balbina, may you live in the Lord,' (i.e. be in paradise with Christ).

SANTA CECILIA
Trastevere

This is one of three important churches neighbouring each other in the Trastevere (trans-Tiber). Even today when urbanization is spreading its mushroom uniformity across the Milvian Bridge (from which Constantine thrust the Emperor Maxentius into the river, with happy results for the Christians), even today, the region retains its distinctive character and its narrow streets reminiscent and redolent of the Orient. An atmosphere that must have predominated in St Cecilia's time, for on that side of the Tiber much merchandise was unloaded from the little ships from Ostia and many of the inhabitants were of Syrian or Jewish nationality.

Far older than its appearance suggests is the church built by Pope Paschal I (817–24) upon the foundations of the house in which the saint was believed to have lived and to have suffered her martyrdom, and where a *titulus* in her name had been established in the third century.

The handsome entrance-hall that precedes the open atrium was raised by Ferdinand Fuga in the eighteenth century. In recent times the atrium, or courtyard, has been arranged as an attractive garden with flower beds round a central fountain whose waters fall into a rectangular basin from the mouth of the ancient catharus that for centuries stood by the convent wall and may even date back to Cecilia's lifetime.

The façade is also a work of Fuga's but the tall bell-tower and the architraved portico are medieval.

The interior of the church is also superficially changed but is structurally as Paschal built it. An attempt to free his marble columns from the concealing piers was unsuccessful for the eighteenth-century plasterers had picked them too deeply. Hap-

Santa Maria in Trastevere

Apsidal mosaic. The central theme, the Triumph of Our Lady in Heaven. This remarkable mosaic marks the return of the art of the mosaist to Rome after a lapse of three hundred years.

Church of Santa Cecilia
Carlo Maderno's sculpture (below the canopy) of th[e] incorrupt body of St Cecilia, buried in the crypt.

Santa Cecilia
Pope Paschal I's apsidal mosaic. He wears the re[c]tangular halo showing that he was alive at the tim[e]. He also carries a model of his church and his mon[o]gram is in the centre of the arch. St Cecilia has [a] protective arm round the Pope's shoulder.

ta Maria in Trastevere

...nded in the fourth century, re-
...t in the twelfth. Upon the
...strade are the figures of four
...es who make an earlier appear-
...e in Pope Innocent II's apsidal
...saic.

a Cecilia

...th-century church. Medieval
...h and tower. Cardinal Sfondrati's
...-of-arms on the façade.

San Vitale
The Martyrdom of St Paphunutis, who was nailed to a tree.

San Vitale
Entrance to the fifth-century church of St Vitalis, now twenty feet

pily, the ninth-century apsidal mosaic; Arnolfo di Cambio's fine thirteenth-century canopy over the high altar and at least some portions of Cavallini's superb frescoes remain.

Cavallini's Fresco of the Last Judgement

An enclosed gallery for the nuns who live in the convent spans the entrance wall and the side walls of the nave. Within the enclosure is a portion of the Last Judgement with its lovely head of Christ. Permission to view this may be obtained from the Superintendent of National Monuments.

Frescoes that date from the fifteenth century have recently been uncovered on the walls of the third chapel on the right-hand side of the nave from the plaster with which they were covered. The chapel nearest to the sanctuary has been newly adorned by the Cardinal-titular who informed the writer (in 1960) that when the floor was taken up more than six hundred bodies had been found. For their souls he had offered many Masses and in return had received great spiritual help and all the money needed to complete his devoted work in the church. 'With love,' he said, 'everything can be achieved; without love, nothing.' Close to this chapel the Cardinal has prepared his own tomb-place; may it be long before it is needed.

The Finding of St Cecilia's Incorrupt Body

With the apsidal mosaic history returns to Pope Paschal. Beneath the sanctuary he had constructed an annular (ring-like) crypt to which he had transferred many bodies from the catacombs. 'Grieved,' he left on record, 'that he could not find the body of St Cecilia,' he returned to the catacomb of St Callistus and there in a crypt that opens from the burial place of the popes, he found a cypress-wood coffin within a recess. In this lay the incorrupt body of the young saint 'clothed in a golden garment with a cloth stained with blood at the feet'.

With great rejoicing the coffin was carried into Rome and after it had been placed in a marble sarcophagus was enshrined beneath the high altar. Seven centuries later, when alterations were in progress around the sanctuary, the sarcophagus and the coffin were opened. The body was still incorrupt and the Roman sculptor, Maderno, was commissioned to carve the lovely recumbent statue that lies under the altar. A plaster cast of the statue has been placed in the recess in the crypt in the catacomb where the coffin had been found.

The Apsidal Mosaic

In Paschal's mosaic the figure of Christ stands upon the clouds of heaven beneath the Hand of God the Father. With his right hand he is making the Greek gesture of blessing: the third finger joined to the thumb. St Peter, St Valerian and St Agatha are on the one side; St Paul, St Cecilia and Pope Paschal, holding a model of his church, on the other side. Paschal has the rectangular halo of the living. The two groups are framed by date-bearing palm trees, signifying paradise. A phoenix, symbol of renewed life is perched in the tree behind St Paul. Early Christian iconography has sometimes intriguing 'side lines', but none without significance. As this mystical bird accompanies St Paul on several occasions its presence is presumably a reference to the Apostle's dissertation, in his Epistle to the Corinthians, on the resurrection of the body (Corinthians I, v. 30-50).

In the zone beneath the human figures, twelve sheep are wending their way to the Lamb of God upon Mount Zion. From the mount flow the four rivers of paradise representing the four gospels of the New Testament. Six of the sheep are coming from the city of Jerusalem, converts from Judaism, and six from Bethlehem, converts from the Gentiles, thus uniting the two parts of Christ's Universal Church.

This theme had made its first appearance in Rome in the fourth century (Mausoleum of Santa Costanza) and in its developed form became popular in apsidal mosaics in the city churches.

The Reconstructed Crypt

In the beginning of the present century Cardinal Rampolla reconstructed the whole area of the crypt and formed within it a large hall-shrine beneath whose altar he placed the sarcophagi of St Cecilia and those of St Valerian and St Tiburtius. Unfortunately this work involved the demolition of ancient substructures with consequential loss of valuable archaeological data.

The hall is resplendent with modern mosaics and is—needless to say—seldom without its eager pilgrims from all nations who come in veneration (*not* worship) to the saint's shrine, as in the fourth century they made their way to her tomb in the catacomb where Pope Damasus (366–84) had to make a secondary exit to ensure their safety.

SANTA MARIA IN TRASTEVERE

Piazza di Santa Maria in Trastevere

Not far from the church of St Cecilia is one described by Professor Frothingham as 'The finest example of the art of the twelfth century in Rome'.[1] Somewhat too exclusive a dictum, for in no other church has art more happily combined one epoch with another.

Historical associations stretch back to primitive times, for Pope Callistus I (217–22) lived in this region where he also suffered his martyrdom at the hands, it is said, of an angry mob who threw him out of a window. Created deacon under Pope Zephyrinus (199–217), Callistus organized for him the Christian cemeteries on the Via Appia and in the catacomb that bears his name he made a crypt for papal tombs, now called by the guides the Chapel of the Popes. The first to lie in it was Zephyrinus, but he was not followed by Callistus for Callistus was buried on the Via Aurelia, a locality nearer his dwelling and probably more convenient at the time of his sudden death.

Either in the lifetime of Pope Callistus or soon after his death there was situated where the church stands a house where the Christians assembled for worship. This was not far from a *taberna meritoria*, an inn with rooms for hire, a place much frequented by sailors on leave from Ravenna. Quarrels were not infrequent between the Christians and the publicans who ran the inn and when a dispute was carried to the Emperor Severus he gave judgement in favour of the former.[2]

[1] Frothingham, loc. cit.
[2] Lampridius, *Alexander Severus*.

The Basilica Built by Pope Julius I

With the advent of religious tolerance Pope Julius I (337–52) replaced the meeting-house with a regular church. This was called alternatively the *titulus Calixti* or the *titulus Julii* but in the early sixth century these titles gave place to the name of Mary, Mother of God, under whose patronage the parish was placed. This may have been owing to influences crossing the river from the great basilica of Santa Maria Maggiore, for devotion to the Mystery of the Incarnation has ever been a bond between the two churches.

In the ninth century, Pope Gregory IV (828–44) repaired and enlarged the ancient church, raising the tribune and extending the crypt beneath it to which he conveyed the relics of Saints Callistus and Cornelius together with those of a martyr-priest, St Calepodius.

Julius' Basilica Rebuilt in the Twelfth Century

Three centuries later, rebuilding became necessary on account of damage caused by earthquake, fire, and the silt deposited by the Tiber. Pope Innocent II (1130–43) built on a larger scale and at a higher level for by that time many old buildings were suffering from humidity and lack of light.

The façade of Innocent's church retains much of its medieval aspect despite Fontana's portico with its effigies of the popes. The mosaic frieze above the windows dates from the late twelfth or early thirteenth century. This reveals interesting changes in the traditional theme and the central figure, the enthroned Madonna, has lost something of the hieratic majesty of past centuries, participating in the coming trend towards the human aspect of her motherhood. Byzantine influence lingers in the poise and solemnity of the two files of virgin-saints holding lighted lamps (symbol of felicity) as they advance to offer homage to the divine Child. These figures are not, as often mistakenly stated, the Wise and Foolish Virgins of the Gospel parable.

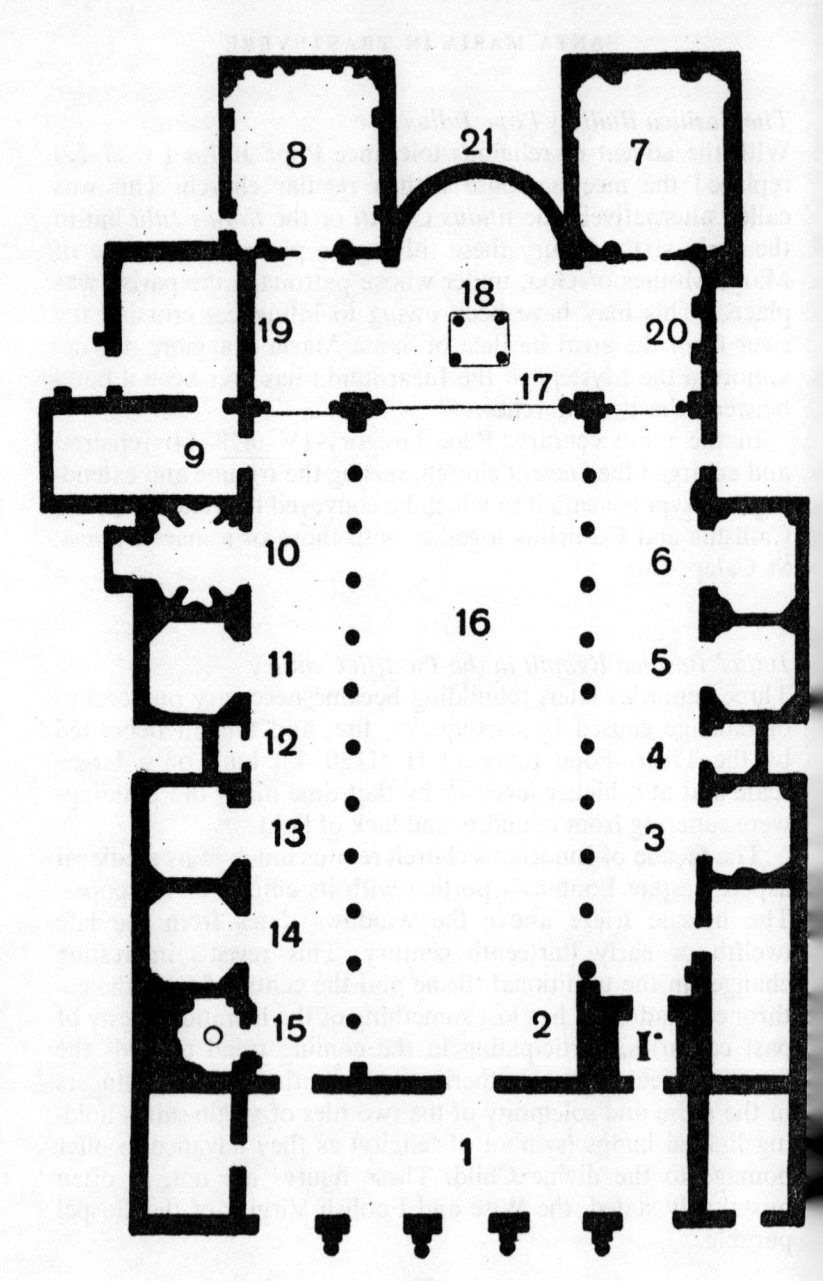

Fig. 13

This mosaic is an important work and has recently undergone restoration.

The splendid interior carries the mind back with a sweep across the centuries. Ancient columns of brown granite support the architraves as they run unbroken to the great triumphal arch. The arch is commanded, as it were, by the two porphyry columns whose magnificent capitals are Roman work of the second century skilfully cut and adapted by the twelfth-century masons. It is said that the columns and their capitals were once in a temple of Isis and that the latter had heads of Egyptian divinities until these were erased at the command of Pope Pius IX (1846–78).

The materials for the beautiful floor of *opus sectile* came from columns of porphyry and other precious marbles. The cost of the floor being shared, in the pleasant custom of the day, by the parishioners, each family contributing so many square feet.

A Remarkable Mosaic in the Apse

The adornment of the apse and of its arch witnesses the return of the art of the mosaicist to Rome, after an interlude of three centuries. The revival came via Monte Cassino when the Abbot sent to Byzantium for artists to beautify his rebuilt abbey.

Fig. 13

Santa Maria in Trastevere
1. Portico remade by Carlo Fontana, eighteenth century. A museum of ancient sculptures and inscriptions.
4. Chapel of the Crib.
6. Chapel with painting of St Peter receiving the keys.
7. The winter chapel of the choir.
8. Chapel of the Blessed Sacrament.
9. Sacristy.
12. Monument of Pope Innocent II.
15. Baptistery.
16. Nave with classical columns and capitals.
18. High altar.
21. In the apse and on the face of the arch mosaics of the time of Pope Innocent II (1130–43).

Those who worked for Pope Innocent II, probably separate Eastern and Romans together, produced a remarkable composition. Upon the arch, beneath the symbols of the Evangelists, the Prophets Isaiah and Jeremiah confront each other. Each points to his scroll with its verses from his prophecy. Upon that of Isaiah: 'Behold, a Virgin shall conceive and bring forth a son.' Upon that of Jeremiah: 'The Lord is held captive in our sins.' This gives the key to an exceptional representation in Christian iconography, a bird in a cage, seen suspended above each scroll. The bird symbolizes the Word (i.e. Jesus Christ, see John I, v. i) captive in the holy womb of Mary.

Within the apse, Christ shares his throne with his mother. His right hand embraces her shoulder; in his left hand is a book open at the words 'Come, My Elect, and share My throne'. Mary holds a scroll with a quotation from the Song of Songs: 'His left hand shall be under my head and his right hand shall uphold me.'

This composition, called *The Triumph of Our Lady in Heaven*, had made its début in a window in the first cathedral of Notre Dame, in Paris. It was there that Pope Innocent could have seen it when he visited Abbot Suger,[1] in whose fertile brain the theme may well have originated.

Around the heavenly throne stand the saints whose relics are venerated in the church, together with the figures of St Peter and Pope Innocent II. None has the attribute of the halo but all have their names between their feet. St Peter characteristically steps forward, while the others are immobile.

Cavallini's Mosaic Panels

The lower part of the apse was afterwards painted by Cavallini with a series of beautiful panels illustrating the life of the Virgin. A detail in the Nativity panel calls for comment. In the foreground, between St Joseph and a shepherd piping to his flock stands a small building accompanied by the words

---

[1] A statesman and historian. During a visit to Rome (1121–22) he was elected Abbot of St Denis. Died 1151.

SS. Marcellino e Pietro

Built by Pope Siricius (384–99). Rebuilt on same site by Pope Benedict XIV (1740–58). 'One of the most striking exteriors in the city.'

San Sisto Vecchio

Fifth-century church with a Baroque façade and a Romanesque tower 'like a forgotten sentinel keeping the centuries at bay'. The convent is adjoining.

San Lorenzo fuori le Mura
Facsimile of the thirteenth-cent
façade and portico destroyed in
war. On the monument St Lawre
holding a gridiron.

San Lorenzo fuori le Mura
Two churches made into one
Pope Honorius III (1216–27).

SANTA MARIA IN TRASTEVERE

taberna meritoria. Was this a reference to the days of Pope Callistus; or had the artist's thought travelled further; to that inn in Bethlehem in which there was no room for the Son of God?

The façade of Santa Maria in Trastevere is sometimes floodlit and the large piazza that confronts it has become a popular rendezvous with the Romans.

SAN VITALE
Via Nazionale

This church was named in the Itinerary of Einsideln as situated *in Vico Longo* and beneath the modern Via Nazionale have been found parts of the pavement that stretched from the Quirinale to the baths of Diocletian.

San Vitale does not usually attract the casual visitor and, more surprisingly, has been neglected until recent years by the antiquarians although listed by Armellini[1] as 'One of the most precious monuments in Rome'. Perhaps the reason is, paradoxically, its position in one of the busiest streets where it is so much below the modern level that little is visible from passing traffic but the tiles of its pent roof!

The Titular Church of St John Fisher
Closer inspection reveals an attractive approach down wide, wall-enclosed steps to a portico now restored to its pristine state by the reopening of immured arches and columns. English pilgrims should descend with alacrity for this was the titular church of St John Fisher. When he was raised to the purple by Pope Paul III in 1534, King Henry VIII is said to have exclaimed: 'Ha! Paul may send him the hat, but I will see that he has no head to set it on.' In later years there grew up a legend in Rome that the Cardinal's body had been secretly conveyed from England and buried in his titular church. But no trace was ever found of the tomb; nor any authentic record.

Built Before the Sack of Rome
Built under Pope Innocent I (401–17), in the years closely pre-

[1] *Le Chiese di Roma*, 1942.

ceding the sack of Rome by Alaric the Goth, San Vitale stood midway between two groups of parish churches: the earlier to the east upon the hills, the later to the west in the plain of the Field of Mars. The foundress was a Roman lady, Vestina, who left instructions in her will that her jewels should be sold and the proceeds given to the Pope for the construction of a church. A request that contrasts with the action of her near-contemporary, the lady Projecta, who buried her treasures in the Esquiline Hill. Church and treasure both survived, the one still serving its original purpose; part of the other, including the famous silver casket, reposing in the somnolent security of the British Museum.

Pope Innocent built the church on the customary basilican plan and dedicated it in the names of St Vitalis and of his putative sons, Saints Gervase and Protase, but it continued for many years to be called the *titulus Vestinae*. The fabric survived many of the disasters that befell the city but after the return of the papacy from Avignon it was in a pitiable state, as were a large number of the smaller city churches. While some were carefully restored, others became quarries for building materials, or were constructively altered.

Reconstruction under Pope Sixtus IV
The inscription above the main door states that Pope Sixtus IV fundamentally restored (*fundamentis restauravit*) the church of St Vitale in the Jubilee Year of 1475. In this so-called 'restoration' the aisles were demolished and the columns replaced by thick walls. This simplified interior thus became a long rectangle with the sanctuary spanning its whole width. The robust columns with their classical capitals that support the pediments of the four side altars are probably survivors from the departed colonnades.

The Paintings in the Nave and in the Apse
In 1598, the church was given by Pope Clement VIII to the Society of Jesus whose novitiate was within easy reach through

adjoining gardens. The new owners lost no time in redecorating the interior to their own taste and their work has survived their long sojourn, as also the return of the church to parish status.

From floor to ceiling the walls are painted with simulated columns and by the figures of prophets standing aloft above landscapes each of which is the background to a scene of martyrdom. The name of the emperor under whom the penalty was inflicted accompanies the episode.

Distressing as this décor may seem to modern susceptibilities the visual impression is mollified by the picturesque rural settings. For instance, St Clement having an anchor attached to his neck is falling without apparent concern into water flowing beneath a bosky verge; the Egyptian hermit, St Paphunutis, although nailed to a tree, seems almost a part of the delicately delineated vista.

More harrowing are two large paintings at the bottom of the nave, which were executed by the Tuscan artist Ciampelli; one depicts St Vitalis stretched upon the rack; the other, his death by stoning. St Vitalis is named in the canon of the Mass in the Milanese Rite and he and his wife St Valeria were probably martyred in the persecution of Marcus Aurelius. The magnificent sixth-century church in Ravenna is dedicated in his name.

Contemporary Portraits in the Apse
Within the apse, Christ is portrayed falling under the weight of the cross. This dramatic picture introduced a number of persons who were possibly painted from the life as they are wearing contemporary clothing, a novelty that had been introduced into art—if Vasari is correct—by the Florentine, Fra Lippo Lippi.

Beneath this central theme is the martyrdom of Saints Gervase and Protase whose bodies had been found near Milan by St Ambrose and rest in the ancient church of San Ambrogolio in that city.

Much of the interest of these paintings lies in the fact that they represent a characteristic phase in the history of religious art in the sixteenth century, i.e. the tendency to instruct; and to beget the desire to emulate the courage and the constancy of the martyrs.

As suggested above, these emotive scenes in San Vitale do not produce a painful ethos but actually one of repose: as though the saints discounted their sufferings, regarding them as gate-money to eternal joy.

SS. MARCELLINO E PIETRO
Via Merulana

At the intersection of two main roads, the Via Merulana and the Via Casilina (the old Via Labicana), stands a four-square church dedicated in the names of two Roman martyrs, St Marcellinus, a priest, and St Peter, an exorcist, commemorated by Pope Damasus (366–84) in one of his metrical epitaphs. In his verses he coupled their names, *'Marcelline e vos pariter Petre posses triumphos'*, and related that in his own boyhood he had heard the details of their martyrdom from the mouth of the executioner. The man had been ordered to bury the bodies secretly but a Christian lady, Lucilla, had discovered the spot and reburied them on the Via Labicana in the catacomb called *'ad duos lauros'*, 'by the two bay trees'.

The Church Built by Pope Siricius
The nucleus of the church was possibly an oratory in the house of St Marcellinus where the formal basilica was erected by Pope Siricius (384–99). Situated as it was in the dip of the valley between two hills the foundations suffered from more or less continual infiltration of running water, with the result that the fabric had repeatedly to be restored.

The Existing Church
Under Pope Benedict XIV (1741–58) the enfeebled building was pulled down and the existing one raised on the site. Its compact plan, that of a Greek cross, and its stepped dome surmounted by a graceful lantern make it one of the most individual and striking exteriors in the city. The interior (a nightmare to photographers) is light and elegant, one arm of the cross being extended to form the sanctuary.

Points of Interest

Above the high altar a large painting by Vaetano Lapis depicts the martyrdom of the titular saints. St Peter is kneeling in prayer while the executioner raises his sword to strike off the head of St Marcellinus. Their faces are serene and joyful.

Upon the right-hand pilaster in the nave is one of the finest epigraphic inscriptions of the thirteenth century, notable for the beauty of the lettering. This enumerates the relics preserved within the altars and the indulgences (remission of punishment still due after sacramental absolution) to be obtained within the octave of the date of the consecration of the church.

Connexion with the Emperor Constantine

There is little else to recall an historical past until, glancing upwards, may be seen in the pendentives of the cupola the Greek monogram, the Chi-Rho, so familiar upon Christian monuments of the fourth century. This awakens the memory of the connexion, actual or devotional, between the Emperor Constantine and his mother, St Helena, with these two saints. It is not impossible that St Helena had known St Marcellinus when he was a young priest in Rome. However that may be, Constantine honoured their memory by building a small basilica above the catacomb where they were buried, and connected it by a stairway to the sepulchral crypt.

St Helena's Mausoleum

Near the entrance to the catacomb the Emperor built an imperial mausoleum where he may at first have planned to be buried. It became St Helena's tomb and her porphyry sarcophagus stood within it until the late Middle Ages when it was removed to the Vatican. Her remains are believed to have been reburied in the church of the Ara Caeli, on the Capitoline Hill; other accounts say they were transported into France. The final resting-place seems uncertain.

The porphyry sarcophagus is now in the Vatican Museum. The core of the mausoleum remains to the present time.

SS. MARCELLINO E PIETRO

The desire to be buried in proximity to a martyr-shrine had become widespread in the fourth century and those who could afford the expense paid large sums to acquire the privilege. In the catacombs, graves were sometimes injured by the introduction of later ones, with this intention. One recalls with admiration Pope Damasus' rejection of his wish to be buried in the papal crypt in the catacomb of Callistus: 'But I feared to disturb the holy ashes of the saints.'

Buried in the same cemetery as Saints Marcellinus and Peter were also the martyrs Saints Gorgonius and Tibertius, the latter the son of Cromatius, a prefect of Rome. All that is known of Gorgonius is that Damasus composed metrical verses in his memory and that he was buried in a crypt upon whose vault there is a faded but important fresco depicting the Lamb of God standing upon Mount Zion acclaimed on the one side by St Peter and St Gorgonius and by Saints Marcellinus and Tibertius on the other side.

In the ninth century the relics of these four martyrs were moved into Rome to the church of SS. Marcellino e Pietro, which then inherited the privileges hitherto accorded to the crypt-chapel in the catacomb.

N.B. Constantine finally made his mausoleum in the church of the Apostles in Byzantium, where his porphyry sarcophagus stood amidst twelve sarcophagi symbolizing the tombs of the twelve Apostles.

SAN LORENZO FUORI LE MURA
Piazzale San Lorenzo

Of the churches built in Rome in honour of the famous deacon, St Lawrence, the most important is situated outside the city walls, as the name implies. It stands above and partly in the catacomb where he was buried. Close by is the vast modern cemetery of the Agro Verano whose tall cypress trees form a picturesque background.

> Graven they look and pious as in copes
> Their dark leaves swathe them.

Since this is the most complex as well as one of the most fascinating of the ancient churches some knowledge of its constructional history is especially helpful.

Constantine the Great did not neglect Rome's 'third patron saint', and built around his grave a crypt-shrine connected by a stairway to a small basilica at surface level, similar in plan to the crypt of Saints Peter and Marcellinus in the catacomb on the Via Libicana.

The basilica was not immediately above the crypt, but a little to the front of it. This detail is not immaterial as it led later on to the moving of the martyr's body.

Two Basilicas, Apse to Apse

A century after its construction the little basilica was unable to accommodate its many pilgrims and Pope Sixtus III (432–40) built a larger church orientated in the opposite direction so that the two buildings stood apse to apse in close proximity, with the larger one covering the tomb-area.

Pope Pelagius II Rebuilds Constantine's Church

Towards the close of the sixth century Constantine's church was in ruins partly because of water seeping in from the hillside and in part as a result of barbarian plunderings. Pope Pelagius II (578–90) rebuilt it, incorporating the classical columns and architraves, and making the foundations secure by digging deeper into the catacomb. In the sanctuary he formed a *matroneum* (women's gallery). This was a normal feature in the architecture of the East but an innovation in the West, where the custom was for the men to stand on the gospel side of the nave and the women on the epistle side.

In his apse Pelagius set a mosaic that is of considerable transitional interest in Christian iconography. Seated upon the globe of the universe, Christ has on His right hand St Peter, St Lawrence, and the Pope carrying a model of the church of which the depicted elevation has intrigued and puzzled the archaeologists. On the other side are St Paul, St Stephen, and St Hippolytus. St Lawrence is taller than the others and wears a golden tunic. Upon his shoulder is his deacon's processional cross and in his hand the book of the gospels. Beneath the main theme comes the dedicatory inscription: 'Since you suffered your martyrdom by fire it is only Just, oh Levite, that light should enter your temples.'

With his work accomplished, the Pope permitted himself a little commendation and added the information that it had been no easy task but one achieved 'With very great difficulty, and amidst the distractions of war'. A reference, presumably, to the noisome Lombards.

The Body of St Lawrence Moved

The distractions, however, did not prevent Pelagius making an important alteration for he moved the body of St Lawrence from its first crypt and placed it within the confession of his church which was known henceforth as the *basilica ad corpus* and the church of Pope Sixtus III, as the *basilica major*.

The moving of a martyr's relics had recently been legalized

but was not to be undertaken without imperial permission. Whether Pope Pelagius fulfilled the letter of the law is problematical, for Justinian was far away in Byzantium, and the times 'were difficult'.

As the centuries passed, both the smaller and the larger church needed restorations and it appears (from data made accessible after the bombing in the 1939–45 war) that the former was rebuilt to a large extent in the early eleventh century still retaining Constantine's columns, capitals, friezes and the architectural feature of the women's gallery.

The Two Churches made into One

Finally, the two separate churches were united into one in the thirteenth century. The two adjacent apses were taken down but the arch with Pope Pelagius' sixth-century mosaic was left intact. This work of unification was probably carried out under Pope Honorius III (1216–27), who built the handsome portico that covered the lower half of the façade. On the inner walls of the portico were frescoes that bore witness to the revival of Italian painting in the era preceding that of Cimabue and Giotto. The porch was destroyed in the war but has been skilfully rebuilt. Of the precious frescoes only fragments remain. Pope Honorius also raised the floor of the smaller basilica which then became the sanctuary, as it is today.

St Lawrence Shares his Tomb with St Stephen

The large crypt beneath the sanctuary is now a well-appointed chapel surrounding the mutual tomb-shrine of St Lawrence and of the protomartyr, St Stephen. When the latter's body was discovered by the priest Lucius near Jerusalem in 415, it was taken to Byzantium and then, at the request of the Empress Eudoxia, transferred to Rome. In the Vatican Library there is a twelfth-century manuscript (Codex. Vat. V. 5696) that incorporated a poem attributed to Pope Pelagius II. This affirms the presence of the relics of St Stephen and that Pelagius had included the protomartyr in his apsidal mosaic.

The Tomb of Pope Pius IX

At the east end of the crypt in a recess that was originally the entrance to Constantine's basilica is the sarcophagus of Pope Pius IX (1846–78), fulfilling his wish to be buried close to the tomb of St Lawrence.

N.B. Two important studies of this remarkable church are included in the Bibliography. That by Professor Muñoz made shortly before the destructive bombing and that by Fra da Bra written shortly after that event.

SAN MARCO
Piazza di San Marco

In the centre of modern Rome embedded within the ample walls of the Palazzo Venetia is the church of St Mark the Evangelist. Its foundation has been ascribed with substantial evidence to the brief papacy of Pope Mark I (Jan.–Oct. 336), who as a priest had laboured long and earnestly under Pope St Sylvester (314–335).

Of Pope Mark it is recorded that in the new and distracting conditions of religious freedom, he did not relax his zeal 'Knowing,' he said, 'that if men cease openly to persecute the Faithful, the devil never allows them any truce.'

In the late Middle Ages the belief arose that this church was built above the house where the evangelist had written his gospel, but it is devoid of historical corroboration. Relics of St Mark and of Pope Mark are under the altar.

Restored by Popes Adrian I and Gregory IV
In its early years the basilica suffered, and survived, the usual vagaries of fortune; was plundered by the marauding Goths and then by the Lombards. More serious injury came from the muddy waters of the Tiber whose overflowings reached to almost incredible distances in the city. The indefatigable restorer of churches, Pope Adrian I (772–95), cleaned and redecorated the interior with loving solicitude for within its walls he had passed many hours of prayer in his boyhood.

Some forty years later Pope Gregory IV (828–44) had to undertake more substantial repairs and carried out the job so thoroughly that the existing building may be said to be his although so changed in appearance that only the apsidal mosaic would be familiar to his eyes were he to return.

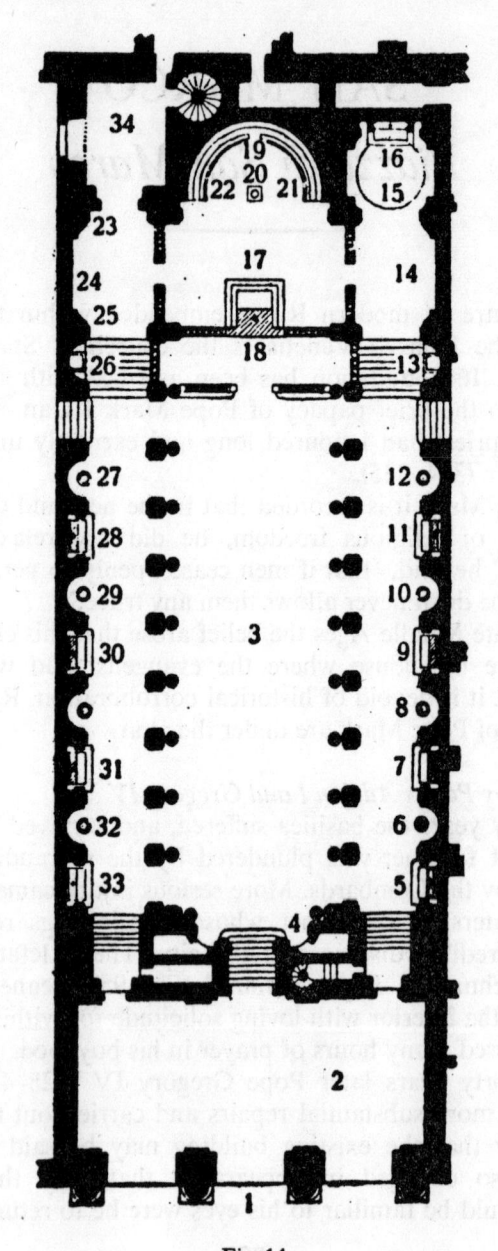

Fig. 14

Architectural Features and Decoration

The entrance is through a handsome double portico erected by Pope Paul II (1464–71), who when he was Cardinal Barbo had built the surrounding palace. The palace had for a time been used as the papal summer residence but afterwards given to the Republic of Venice for the Venetian ambassador.

To Pope Paul is also due the large circular-headed windows in the nave and the magnificent hammered ceiling inserted after the roof had been covered with lead tiles, one of which, marked with his stamp, is in the chapter house.

Other major alterations date chiefly to the eighteenth century. Notable is the curious arrangement of columns made of brick veneered with red Silician jasper set in front of the piers. The stucco reliefs in the zone above the piers illustrate activities in the lives of the Apostles. They alternate with fresco panels of various themes. Those on the right-hand side depict the martyrdom of the Persians, Saints Abdon and Sennen.

Ninth-century Mosaics in the Apse

With the changed aspect of the nave, Pope Gregory's mosaics in the apse shine like antique jewels in a bizarre setting. The austere Christ standing upon a pedestal gives his blessing in the Greek manner (the third finger of the right hand joined to the thumb) while holding in the left hand a book bearing the declaration: 'I am the Light; the Way; the Resurrection.'

Above Christ's head the hand of God the Father holds a

Fig. 14

San Marco
1. Handsome double porch (with loggia for papal benedictions). Erected by Paul II (1464–71).
3. Magnificent hammered ceiling, fifteenth century.
15. Chapel of the Blessed Sacrament, by Pietro da Cortona.
18. Porphyry urn containing the body of Pope St Mark.
19. Ninth-century mosaics in the apse.
32. Baptistery.
34. Sacristy. Descent to the crypt.

crown and below Christ's feet is the Dove of the Holy Spirit, and together they form the symbol of the Trinity.

The alignment of the accompanying saints is rather a surprising one. On the left of Christ is Pope Mark I vested as a bishop; next comes the young deacon Agapitus and finally St Agnes. On the Lord's right hand is the deacon St Feliciamus who, with St Agapitus, was executed under the Emperor Valerian in 258. Accompanying Feliciamus is St Mark the Evangelist 'introducing' Pope Gregory who holds the model of his church and has the square halo. All stand upon pedestals bearing their names.

Historically and artistically these mosaics are a landmark. Historically, because they commemorate the end of the iconoclastic struggle between the papacy and Byzantium. Artistically, because they were the last to appear in a Roman church for the next three hundred years.

These spiritualized figures, icons rather than persons, have in the past been decried as exemplifying the artistic decadence of the era. Such a judgement is too superficial for it was the artist's intention to give them an unearthly aspect to emphasize the difference between their material state and their spiritual. Byzantine craftsmen were bound by stringent rules but these helped rather than hindered their religious purpose, which was to lead the beholder to look *through* the images as well as *at* them; seeing them as aids to prayer and contemplation.

Frescoes in the Crypt

In 1843 the crypt was opened after a long period of closure and upon one wall was a ninth-century fresco showing Christ with Saints Abdon and Sennen and St Hermes. The two former had come to Rome in 250 and died for their Faith in the Colosseum. Of St Hermes little is recorded beyond the fact of his martyrdom and of his burial on the Old Salarian Way. The relics of these saints and those of the deacons in the apsidal mosaic had all been brought into the church by Pope Gregory.

The plan of the crypt differs from the annular type. A quadrilateral gallery leads to the Altar of the Relics and from there semi-circular passages, with niches for lamps, open out. Copies of the earthenware lamps used in the catacombs have been placed in the niches.

Permission to visit the crypt is obtained from the sacristan, whose bell (very inconspicuous) is in the porch.

SANTA PUDENZIANA
Via Urbana

Upon entering this famous church the pilgrim comes close to the roots of Christianity in Rome, intimately connected as was its foundation with the senatorial family with whom St Peter is traditionally believed to have stayed in the early days of his ministry.

If that is correct, St Peter's hosts were the senator Pudens and his wife Priscilla, owners of considerable property in the district.[1] Their son, Pudens the Younger, married Claudia Rufina (both mentioned by St Paul in his second epistle to Timothy), who became the parents of two sons, Timotheus and Novatus, and possibly of two daughters, Pudenziana and Prassede, but the actual relationship of these last is debatable.

That the local Christians gathered for worship in the Pudens' house is quite probable, but the first separate building for the cult was a small hall-church formed into part of adjacent thermal baths in the time of Pope Pius I (141–55). This was called the *titulus Pudentis*. Its subsequent history is obscure and historical data only return with Pope Innocent I (401–17), who erected the existing basilica on the site and introduced the title *Ecclesia Pudenziana*, although some years later a cleric was still signing himself '*Asterius presbytr tituli Pudentis*' (Asterius, cleric of the title Pudentis).

The Present Aspect of the Basilica
Facing the Via Urbana (the ancient Vicus Patricius) the church is now partly below street level with its approach across a courtyard from a dignified stairway constructed by Cardinal

[1] H. Marucchi, *Basiliques et églises de Rome*.

Lucien Bonaparte in 1870. The façade was then refashioned and its frescoes, recently repainted, depict St Peter enthroned between 'Saint' Pudens and 'Saint' Pudenziana, Pope Pius I and Pope Gregory VII (1073–85).

The central doorway, believed to have been given by Pope Gregory (the great Hildebrand), was fortunately retained. In the medallions of its frieze are busts of Pudenziana, of Prassede, of Pudens and of Pastor, an enigmatic character whose connexion with the church has been variously interpreted. The style of the carving is reminiscent of eleventh-century German miniatures and the frieze is held to be one of the most important medieval sculptures in Rome.

The Interior of the Basilica

The interior of the basilica is seen to advantage on a sunny morning when the main door is open to permit a glimpse from the threshold of the grand mosaic in the apse.

Closer inspection reveals that the nave walls have been stripped in places to show the original brickwork and some of the columns. A gap in the floor permits a view of the substructure where galleries of ninth-century date have been opened. In one gallery is a well-preserved fresco of St Peter with Santa Potentiana and Santa Prassede, whose names run vertically at their sides.

The vaulted ceiling in the nave was raised in the sixteenth century. The eliptical dome set transversely over the sanctuary is an architecturally interesting feature that seems to have become fashionable in Rome in the Baroque era, although of ancient ancestry in the architecture of the East.

The apsidal mosaic is a masterpiece of fifth-century Roman art. Its architectural setting aroused much discussion in the past, but it is now generally conceded that the buildings in the background were parts of the fourth-century scene in Jerusalem and include Constantine's Rotunda of the Holy Sepulchre and one façade of the Martyrium. The cross on the mount figures the cross of gold placed by Constantine upon Calvary.

In the foreground the majestic, bearded Christ sits amongst

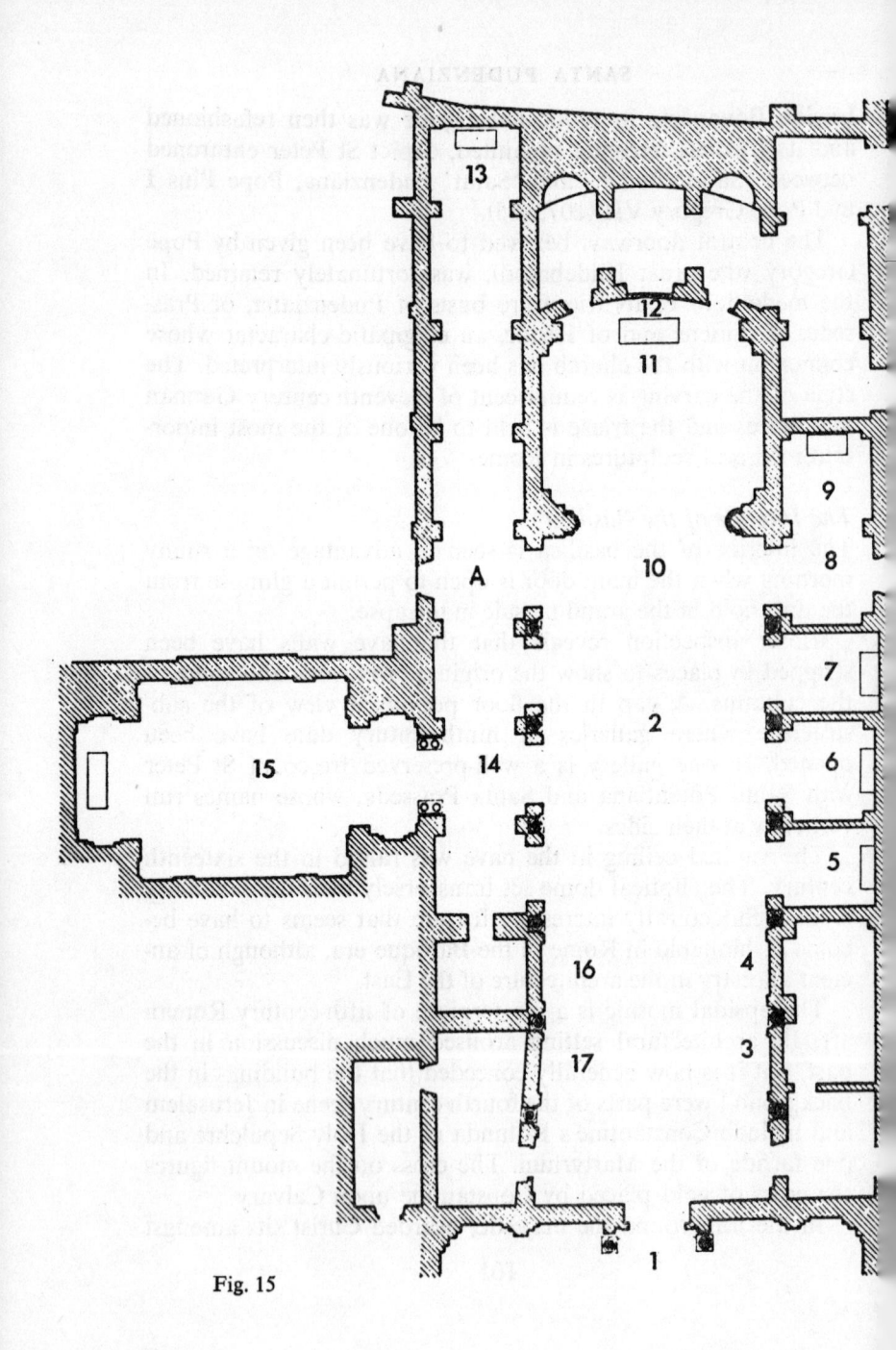

Fig. 15

his Apostles. The female figures holding crowns or wreaths over the heads of St Peter and St Paul are not, as formerly supposed, the sisters Pudenziana and Prassede, but symbolize the Church of the Jews and that of the Gentiles.

The full-scale composition of this splendid work was truncated when a new arch was put up; but it remains outstanding.

Attached to the left-hand aisle but external to it, with its small portico in the Via Balbo, is a charming oratory of Our Lady. Upon one wall is a medieval fresco of the Madonna and Child between St Pudenziana and St Prassede. The clothing is that of ladies of middle rank, with yellow the predominating shade. A copy of the fresco is in the library at Windsor.

This little sanctuary—one of the small delights of Rome—is not open to the public, but is seen satisfactorily through its window in the Via Balbo.

Fig. 15
Santa Pudenziana
1. Façade. Door surmounted by eleventh-century marble entablature with medallions.
2. Fifth-century interior refashioned in 1588. Ancient columns are visible in the side walls.
10. Elliptical cupola inserted in sixteenth century.
12. Early fifth-century mosaic in the apse.
15. The Caetani Chapel, sixteenth century.
A. Entrance to a charming oratory situated in the adjacent Via Balbo. Important eleventh-century frescoes.

SANT' AGATA DEI GOTI
Via Mazzarino

In the special Holy Year of 1933 Pope Pius XI (1922–39) accorded to the church of St Agatha of the Goths[1] the privilege of sharing with that of St Pudenziana the Lenten Station on the Tuesday in the third week in Lent.

This church, where relics of St Agatha are honoured, was the principal one of the Gothic-Arian Community in Rome and was under the patronage of the famous barbarian administrator and general, Ricimer, who in the decade 460–70 adorned the apse with a mosaic which was *in situ* for over a millennium. It was called 'Ricimer's church' and he was buried in it; as later on was a man named Mesina whose funerary inscription called down upon profaners of his tomb the maledictions of 'The four Evangelists and the three hundred and eighteen Fathers of Nicea'!

St Agatha was not herself concerned in any known way with the Gothic peoples. She lived in Catania (Sicily) where for her rejection of the amorous advances of the governor, Quintain, she was arrested on the charge of being a Christian and after suffering terrible torments died of her wounds in prison.

That she was venerated in Rome is apparent from her appearing in several apsidal mosaics in the city and her name is in the canon of the Roman Mass.

The Church Reconsecrated
At the close of the sixth century, after forty years of neglect, the church was taken into Catholic use and reconsecrated by

---
[1] As this is not a parish church, it is normally closed to the public after the early Mass, until 5.30 p.m.

Pope Gregory the Great, who placed relics of St Agatha and of St Sebastian beneath the high altar.

Described in ancient documents as situated *'in capite Suburae'*, it stands at the junction of the Via Panisperna and the Via Mazzarino, concealed on the corner by its attached House of Studies, in the possession of the Stigmatine Fathers. The unpretentious façade faces the Via Mazzarino and opens to an irregular forecourt surrounded by porticoes.

On plan, the form is basilican with semi-circular apse and a slightly raised sanctuary. The aisles are defined by arcading supported upon red granite columns. Three rectangular windows interspaced with episodes from the life and death of St Agatha pierce the clerestory walls on either side.

At first glance the red granite columns alone seem to bear witness to antiquity, but careful examination has shown this to be misleading. The masonry is similar to that of other Roman churches of the fifth century, but the nave is narrower than the norm while the aisles are enlarged. Hollow tiles in the half-dome of the apse and the arrangement of the original windows indicate influences foreign to early Christian tradition in Rome. (An attractive view of the exterior may be obtained through a door in the right-hand aisle.) Moreover, none of the measurements can be translated into round figures of Roman feet; but if the Byzantine foot-measure is used the result works out in round figures. As Professor Krautheimer, who made this survey, states:

'One might wonder whether this Byzantine influence on Sant' Agata dei Goti was owing to the fact that the basilica was founded by a Gothic community in close contact with the East through its Arian faith, or whether this indicates a general near-eastern current which from the middle of the fifth century was always on the increase in Rome.'[1]

---

[1] R. Krautheimer, *Corpus Basilicarum Christianarum Romae*, 1937.

The Greek Martyrs

An important possession of the church is that of a large number of relics of the saints known as the Greek Martyrs. This famous group had been accustomed to meet in one of the crypts of a catacomb on the Via Appia during the persecution of Valerian (258), there to study together the holy scriptures. After their martyrdom they were buried together and their sepulchre became a place of pilgrimage, as recorded in several texts including that of the seventh-century Itinerary of Malmesbury. When the bodies (sewn into linen sacks) were removed from the catacomb in the ninth century they were brought to this church, where they rested undisturbed until the sixteenth century at which date Cardinal Barberini had the reliquaries opened and the bones put into two lead caskets. One was then placed beneath the high altar and the other in the chapel of St Agatha, at the head of the right-hand aisle.

Such was the disposition when Carlo Resphighi, Secretary to the Pontifical Institute of Sacred Archaeology, discovered them when the altars were reconstructed in 1932. In the Holy Year of 1933, Cardinal Bisletti caused the relics to be carried in procession over the ground where the martyrs had suffered their glorious witness. Returned to the church, they were replaced beneath the altars, but some of the relics remain exposed in a wall-reliquary in St Agatha's chapel.

The linen sacks, or shrouds, inscribed in the ninth century with the saints' names, are in the Museo Sacro in the Vatican.

A full account of these martyrs is given in *Rivista Di Archeologia Cristiana*, 1933.

SAN SISTO VECCHIO
Piazzale Numa Pompilio

'When I came out from San Sisto Vecchio the wind from the sea had dispersed the clouds and at the top of the Palatine the ruins of the palace of Septimus Severus stood out against a blue sky. I was thinking that the convent of Saint Sixtus which receives so few visitors was one of the privileged places where the thirteenth century still survived. Little, indeed, remains but the imagination evokes that which is no longer visible. The more one knows, the more one enjoys the beauties of Rome. Study brings to life the churches when a first visit has revealed little. Saint Sixtus is one example amongst many.'[1]

The church received its appellation 'Old' in the sixteenth century, when another church, dedicated in the name of Pope Sixtus II (257–58), was built on the Quirinale. The original title was the *titulus Tigridae*, so called after its fifth-century foundress. Connexion with the martyred Pope Sixtus is owing to a delightful medieval legend. This relates that when Sixtus was being led to execution he encountered his deacon, St Lawrence, on this spot and the latter cried in consternation: 'Father where are you going without your son? Priest, where go you without your deacon?' Sixtus made reply: 'My son, I will not abandon you...a great conflict awaits you...you will follow me in three days' time.'

Architectural Alterations
From its fifth-century form, that of a three-aisled basilica with an apse but no transept, the church was reduced to a single nave by Pope Innocent III (1198–1216), whose Romanesque

[1] E. Mâle, *Rome et ses vieilles églises*.

tower rises above the orange-tinted Baroque façade. But it is the façade, not the tower, that is anachronistic for when that is penetrated, time reverts.

Connexion with St Dominic

Response to a bell by a side-door brings a nun in the Dominican habit and the visitor steps into the cloister. This opens on the right-hand side, to the splendid Chapter House where St Dominic was wont to gather and instruct his disciples. The Community now use it as their chapel.

The refectory still fulfils its normal function and has not materially changed since St Dominic and his hungry brethren sat before the empty tables on a day when there was no money with which to buy food.

'The Religious looked for a while in surprise at the empty plates and cups and then at St Dominic who was praying, his hands being joined together on the table. Suddenly two angels appeared in the midst of the refectory carrying loaves on two white cloths. They began to distribute the bread, beginning at the lower end of the tables, placing before each Brother one whole loaf of white, exquisite bread. When they were come to Saint Dominic they placed in like manner an entire loaf before him, then bowed their heads and disappeared.'[1]

Pope Honorius III (1216–27), who was a strong supporter of Dominic, had given the church of San Sisto Vecchio with its monastery to the Friars, but when he needed the property for another purpose he gave them in its place the more healthily situated church of Santa Sabina on the Aventine Hill and built a monastery to adjoin it, within the ramparts of a fortress-castle which he possessed.

However, this change of location did not sever St Dominic's connexion with his former home. It was the Pope's purpose to move to San Sisto Vecchio from their convent in Rome a com-

[1] Drane, *Life of St Dominic*.

SAN SISTO VECCHIO

munity of nuns whose way of life required reforming, and it was to be St Dominic's task to carry that out.

Before consenting to this material and moral translation the 'reformees' made a condition that they should take with them the famous icon of the Madonna which for years had been venerated in their chapel. If the icon 'settled' in its new home, they would do the same. St Dominic agreed. At midnight (to avoid popular interference) a procession walking barefoot and carrying torches accompanied the sacred picture to San Sisto. All went happily and on Ash Wednesday of the year 1221 Dominic received the vows of his new daughters, for whom he composed a Rule based, with some additions, upon that of St Augustine. Within a short time the Community came to number sixty strong.

The Nuns Move to Rome, and Back Again

By the sixteenth century the countryside around the lower reaches of the Aventine was almost completely deserted, as the district was afflicted with malaria. Pope Pius V (1566–72) moved the nuns to the new convent of SS. Dominic and Sixtus close to the Piazza Magnanapoli in Rome. In 1872, their property was confiscated by the government and made into a secular school. And the Dominican Sisters returned to San Sisto Vecchio.

SS. COSMA E DAMIANO
Forum Romanum

In the heart of ancient Rome, close to the Roman Forum and bordering the *Via Sacra*, is the picturesque church dedicated in the names of Saints Cosmas and Damian, brothers and physicians martyred in Cilicia in the reign of Diocletian. Together with St Luke they are the patron saints of doctors and their names are in the canon of the Mass. For refusing to take fees from their patients they were nicknamed 'the silverless ones' and have remained popular figures in religious art throughout the centuries. After their death many miracles of healing were wrought through their intercession, including a cure of the Emperor Justinian who in gratitude built a church in their honour in Byzantium.

Two Pagan Buildings Converted into a Church
The exceptional character of the church in the *Via Sacra* is owing to the circumstance that it was converted by Pope Felix IV (526–30), from two mutually-adjacent pagan buildings; a circular one (*heroon*) built in the fourth century by the Emperor Maxentius in memory of his son Romulus,[1] and the rectangular *Templum Almae Urbis*, a civic hall where the archives of the censor and the municipal plans were kept.

Although small Christian oratories had frequently been inserted into disused pagan buildings, this was the earliest adaptation of such buildings into a church, and to accomplish it Pope Felix had to ask permission from the Gothic King, Theodoric, then governing Rome. Happily, time has but little changed the exterior aspect. Even the porphyry columns and

[1] The circular *heroon* is no longer used as narthex to the church but houses a famous Neapolitan crib.

the marble architraves of the *heroon* are extant, although it is remarkable that they have not been 'borrowed'.

The plan adopted for the conversion was of the simplest; the circular building became the vestibule and the rectangular hall the nave. At the far end of the latter an apse was raised upon arches, the space at the rear being used as a sacristy, as it is to this day.

A Magnificent Mosaic
Felix permitted the marble intaglio hunting scenes to remain on the walls of the nave but adorned his apse with a masterly composition in mosaic. The theme of this became the prototype for apsidal mosaics in Roman churches where the titular saints are 'introduced' to Christ by St Peter and St Paul.

Although Baroque interpolations have mutilated the full-scale composition with the Four-and-Twenty Elders on the arch adoring Christ, the mosaic remains one of the most impressive monuments of Christian art. Upon a pathway of clouds Christ descends, with a wide gesture of oratory, his right arm extended and in his left hand the scroll of his doctrine. From the green banks of the Jordan, St Peter 'introduces' St Damian, and St Paul performs the same office for St Cosmas. The martyrs carry their victor's crowns ('Be thou faithful unto death and I will give thee a crown of life'). From their wrists hang their satchels of surgical instruments.

St Peter's Tonsure and St Paul's Phoenix
St Peter's characteristically thick and curly hair is shorn and his head encircled with the full tonsure known as the Petrine, in distinction from the semi-tonsure of the magician Simon Magus. In the palm-tree behind St Paul is his phoenix, symbol of the resurrection of the body. The groups are closed by Pope Felix holding the model of his church; and by St Theodore. The figure of the former is a restoration, disproportionately tall, and is said to have been given the features of Pope Urban VIII, the pontif responsible for the reorganization of the church in the seventeenth century.

SS. COSMA E DAMIANO

St Theodore, called affectionately St Toto by the Romans, was put to death by Maximian in 306. His panegyric pronounced by St Gregory of Nyssa contains the exhortation: 'O, Theodore, as soldier defend us; as martyr intercede for us, obtain for us peace... stir up [sic] St Peter and St Paul that they may be solicitous for the churches they founded.'

This warrior-saint has his own sixth-century church, on the far side of the Palatine Hill.

The Middle Ages
In the early Middle Ages the Palatine and its immediate surroundings had considerable ecclesiastical importance. Neglected by the emperors in Byzantium, Rome had declined politically and numerically, and civic as well as religious administration had devolved to a large extent upon the papacy. At that period the popes were living in part of a deserted palace on the Palatine opposite the church of SS. Cosma e Damiano, to which they made substantial gifts.

Later on, the political and social life of the city shifted to the other side of the Capitol. Earthquakes and floods changed the level of the ground and many of the smaller churches had to be abandoned. Pope Felix's church was more fortunate and continued in use until the prevailing humidity rendered it too unhealthy.

Restored in the Seventeenth Century
Pope Urban VIII (1623–44) undertook a thorough restoration. He closed up the entrance from the Via Sacra and inserted a new floor at a higher level, thus creating two churches. The upper church (the only part now used for services) is compact and pleasing, with its coffered and gilded ceiling and handsome marble floor of unusual design and colour, enclosing Urban's coat-of-arms. But the striking feature is still the sixth-century mosaic in the apse, now exceptionally easy to inspect owing to the raised floor.

SAN LORENZO IN LUCINA
Piazza di San Lorenzo in Lucina

The church of St Lawrence in Lucina stands in the piazza of that name bounded at one end by the Corso. Some antiquarians have thought that the name derived from a temple of Juno Lucina converted to Christian use but at the date of its foundation no such conversion of temples into churches had been undertaken; nor would the form of building suggest it.

The title was the *titulus Lucinae* in the fourth century and the remains of a house uncovered behind the apse may well have been the home of a foundress named Lucina.

It was a church of sufficient importance for the election of Pope Damasus I (366–84) to have taken place within its walls. Pope Sixtus III (432–40) carried out extensive restorations and in the sixth century it was listed with the Stational churches.

Architectural Additions and Changes
The façade, the bell-tower, and the porch as they exist today all date from the time of Pope Paschal II (1099–1118). The work then carried out must have included much of the fabric, since the anti-pope Anacletus II thought reconsecration to be necessary and on May 25, 1130 performed the ceremony. His inscription in the porch enumerates the names of the martyrs whose bodies he had placed beneath the altars, together with two glass phials containing 'blood and fat' (*et adipe*) 'of the blessed martyr Lawrence'. It concludes with a reference to another major relic, that of the gridiron upon which St Lawrence had suffered his martyrdom.

The consecration by Anacletus was declared null and void, like all his sacerdotal actions, by the Lateran Council in 1135, and San Lorenzo in Lucina was eventually brought back into

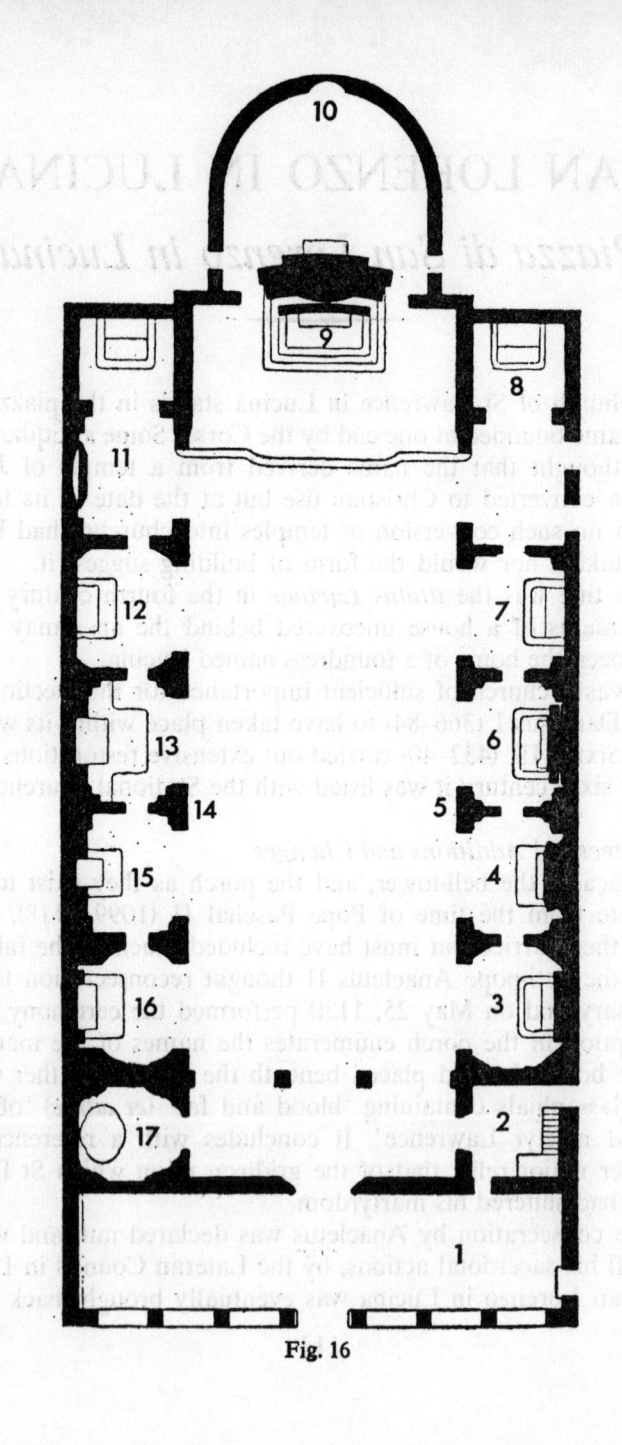

Fig. 16

n Marco

ounded by Pope Mark I (Jan.–Oct. 336). Rebuilt by Pope Gregory IV in ninth century. Interior constructed in eighteenth century.

n Marco

e apsidal mosaic of Pope Gregory IV.

Santa Pudenziana

Fourth-century nave. Eleventh-century doorway with important sculptured entablature. Romanesque bell-tower; nineteenth-century façade.

Santa Pudenziana

Apsidal mosaic contemporary with the nave. Christ enthroned. Background of Constantinian buildings, Jerusalem.

the fold (like a lapsed member) by Pope Celestine III, whose inscription, also in the porch, commemorates *his* reconsecration in 1195 as a ceremony attended by 'The archbishops of York, of Acerenza, of Siponte and great numbers of Romans and Others'.

Mention of the Archbishop of York calls to mind the name of another Englishman, Hugo Atratus of Evesham, who was cardinal titular of the church in 1260. On account of his medical skill the Cardinal was nicknamed 'the phoenix of doctors'. He was the first English student at the medical college in Padua.

The Chapel of St Lawrence

The interior of the church was remodelled in the seventeenth century and its wide nave, flanked by intercommunicating chapels, is reminiscent, on a small scale, of the plan of the Gesu, the principal church of the Jesuits in Rome.

The first chapel on the right-hand side is that of St Lawrence. Beneath its altar is a crystal reliquary holding the gridiron, now no more than an iron bar. This famous relic was brought here after the destruction of a church called San Lorenzo della Craticola (St Lawrence of the gridiron, or grating) where it had long been preserved.

Points of Interest

In the centre of the coffered and gilded ceiling is a painting of

Fig. 16
San Lorenzo in Lucina
1. Portico built by Pope Paschal II (1099–1118).
2. Romanesque bell-tower.
3. Chapel of St Lawrence.
4. Chapel of the Blessed Sacrament.
5. Bust of Nicholas Poussin.
8. Chapel of the Crucifix.
9. High altar, Guido Reni's Crucifixion.
10. *Cathedra* of Pope Paschal II (1099–1118).
16. Chapel of St Charles Borromeo.
17. Baptistery.

the Ascension of Christ in the presence of St Lawrence, Pope Damasus, Lucina, and St Francis Caracciolo. The introduction of the last-named is difficult to explain. Caracciolo (1563–1608) had joined the Order called Clerks Regular, who lived penitential lives and gave missions throughout Italy. He became superior-general, but his connexion here is not self-evident.

The nave has some fine Baroque sculpture and a monument to Nicholas Poussin, a gift of Chateaubriand's. Poussin's painting of St Bernard leading the anti-pope Anacletus to the feet of Pope Innocent II is in the church of Santa Croce.

The somewhat massive high altar with its fluted columns of black marble is graced with Guido Reni's very beautiful Crucifixion. This is often veiled but the sacristan will uncover it upon request. At the same time he should be asked to unlock a recess in the centre of the panelling in the apse, where a marble throne that belonged to Pope Paschal II is concealed. Its sides are composed of marble of the Roman imperial epoch carved with vine leaves. Upon the front and back runs a lengthy inscription in Latin to the effect that in the year 1112 the gridiron and the glass phials were under the high altar.

Among the martyrs whose relics are preserved in the church are those of Pope Pontianus (230–35), who died of his sufferings in the mines of Sardinia, and of St Vincent, a deacon, who under Dacian, governor of Spain, was roasted alive for refusing to deny Christ. For which reason his name follows that of St Lawrence in the Litany of the Saints.

SANTA SUSANNA
Piazza S. Bernardo

The church that bears the name of Saint Susanna, virgin and martyr, is the national church of the large American colony in Rome.

To the architect sensitive to purities of style it is intriguing, for the grand Baroque façade, designed by Maderno, is not integrated with the body of the building behind it. Rather it is reminiscent of a mask concealing an ancient face. It covers both the width of the nave and the front of the adjoining sacristy and of a corresponding room on the other side. The upper half consists of three parts flanked by pilasters with two outer wings. The lower has five parts, the quiet, restful breadth of which balances with strength and stability the soaring verticality of the centre. The four statues in the recesses are those of Pope St Caius and St Gabinius; of St Susanna and St Felicity.

For the archaeologist, interest lies in the remains of the third-century mansion, believed to have been the home of St Gabinius and his daughter Susanna, over which the church was built.

According to tradition, Susanna had refused to marry Galerius, the adopted son of the Emperor Diocletian, to whom her family were related. This refusal resulted in the martyrdom of the saint and of her father, Gabinius, and possibly (but questionably) of her uncle Pope Caius (283–96), who was buried in the catacomb of Callistus where his epitaph was unearthed and set up again by de Rossi.

The church probably dates from the fourth century, but the earliest existing record is found in the year 497. A century later Pope Gregory the Great named it the titular Church of Saint Susanna. It was rebuilt to a large extent in the ninth century, as shown by the brickwork. This took place under Pope Leo III (795–816), who adorned the apse with a mosaic depicting Christ enthroned between Charlemagne and his own image holding a model of his church. Both figures had the square halo, which indicated that the person represented was still alive.

The Sixteenth Century
In the sixteenth century the interior was materially altered. An elaborate ceiling was inserted and the nave walls covered with heroic-sized paintings by Baldassare Croce of episodes in the life of the chaste Susanna of the Old Testament. These are divided by flat pilasters supporting at ceiling level statues of the prophets Ezechiel, Daniel, Isaiah and Jeremiah. The chapel opening from the nave on the right hand is the chapel of the crucifixion; opposite is the chapel of St Lawrence, where relics of St Genesius, patron saint of actors, are preserved. Genesius is said to have composed a comedy parodying Christian baptism, but was converted while performing in this blasphemous act. His statue is amongst those with which Bernini crowned his glorious colonnade around the piazza of St Peter's basilica.

In the sanctuary Susanna is seen accompanied by female figures symbolizing Religion and the Church. Beneath these substantial figures, Martyrdom carries the cross of penitence; the crown of thorns; and the bitter chalice of suffering. In the background are many of the instruments used in torturing the early Christians.

This church has been called 'a Baroque jewel of a grandiose century', but the spirit that breathes within it is not 'grandiose'. On the contrary, it exhales in a marked degree charity and the spirit of faith in action.

A double stairway leads to the crypt where relics of Saint Susanna, Saint Gabinius, Saint Felicity and Saint Silanus (sometimes written Silvanus) are preserved. Felicity and Silanus are authenticated martyrs and were buried close together in the catacomb of Massimus. In the legendary fifth-century Acts of Saint Felicity she is stated to have been the mother of Silanus and of six other sons all of whom were martyred before her eyes; herself the last to suffer. The reliability of this account has been hotly disputed. On the credit side is the epitaph composed by Pope Damasus and references of other fourth-century writers; in the eulogies of St Augustine and in the references of Pope Gregory the Great to the martyrdoms. So the matter stands.

Excavations made in 1880 uncovered part of the third-century floor and of a wall.

SANTA CROCE IN GERUSALEMME
Porta Maggiore

The church of the Holy Cross, a near neighbour to the Lateran Basilica, is situated in a region comparatively recently urbanized but formerly commanding one of the most poetic vistas in Rome. A note in the diary of Cardinal Manning makes mention of the locality: 'Went with St John to Santa Croce, a fine spacious convent, very clean and well kept, with beautiful views upon the Alban Hills to Tivoli with Frascati in the middle. Saw Newman in his chamber, which looks on this view.'

St Helena Sets Out to Find the True Cross

In the early fourth century, when St Helena, Mother of Constantine the Great, set out in her old age for Jerusalem, the district was known as the Sessorianum, with a city gate of that name, now the Porta Maggiore. It was all imperial property and included a palace where the Empress-Mother dwelt.

Save for the circumstance of her advanced years, St Helena was not undertaking a very exceptional enterprise in making a journey to the Holy Places in Palestine, for many Christians were doing the same, some as a penance for their sins, many from devotion. What *was* remarkable was her inspiration to seek for the True Cross (and her perseverance in the search), for the Mount of Calvary had long since been buried beneath Hadrian's Temple to Venus.

When the beams of the cross were at last discovered, in a disused cistern, St Helena arranged with the Bishop of Jerusalem, St Macarius, for a church to be built upon Calvary. Constantine developed the scheme and built the *Martyrium* (a church built over a martyr's remains or over the place of the martyrdom) and the adjoining Basilica-of-the-Resurrection and thus covered and consecrated the whole area.

Her task accomplished, St Helena returned to Rome, taking in the baggage-train a large portion of the Cross and many tons of earth from Calvary. Part of the Sessorian palace was then made into a church by adding an apsidal sanctuary to the audience hall and by dividing its interior by two transverse walls. A room adjoining the hall became a private chapel and upon its floor was spread the earth from Calvary. This is called St Helena's chapel and above the altar is the Empress-Mother's statue, 'converted', according to Lanciani, from one of the goddess Juno by the substitution of a new head and a cross placed in her hand.[1]

The church in the palace was known at first as *Sancta Hierusalem* or, alternatively, the *Basilica Heleiana*. A century later the title had become *Basilica Sanctae Crucis* although as late as the eighth century reference to *Sancta Hierusalem* may be found.

When the roof fell in Pope Gregory II (715–31) replaced it, and to that time may be attributed the introduction of the side aisles.

A Monastery Added in the Tenth Century
Pope Benedict VII (974–83) added a monastery for the Benedictines who moved in from the Lateran. The Pope had his tomb in the church and his epitaph to the poor may be read in the main entrance.

Pope Lucius II (1144–45) brought the exterior of the building into conformity with the prevailing Romanesque style by the addition of a portico, a bell-tower and cloisters, and adorned the interior with frescoes, of which important remains were accidentally uncovered in 1913.

During the Avignonese exile of the papacy, the general

[1] Lanciani, *Wanderings in Roman Churches*.

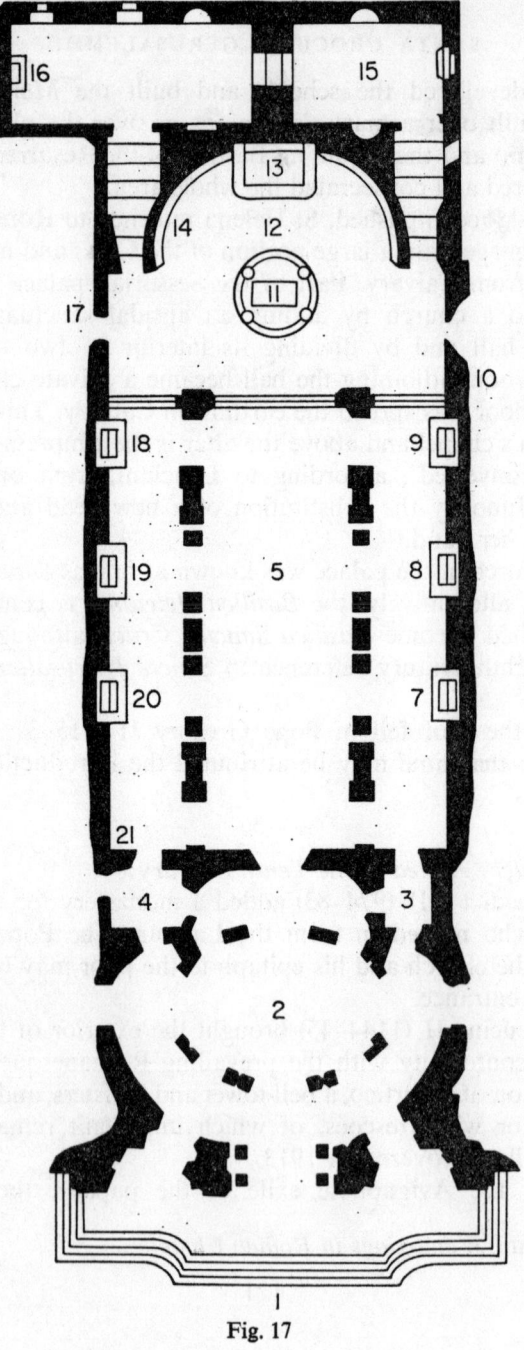

Fig. 17

SS. Cosma e Damiano
Two pagan buildings converted into a church by Pope Felix IV (526–30).

SS. Cosma e Damiano
Pope Felix's glorious apsidal mosaic. Christ descending the clouds of heaven. SS. Peter and Paul 'introduce' the martyrs.

San Lorenzo in Lucina

Built above the house of the lady Lucina in mid-fourth century. The interior re-styled in eighteenth century. Guido Reni's famous crucifixion behing the altar. The first chapel on the right-hand side contains a reliquary with a bar from S Lawrence's gridiron.

Santa Susanna

Church built above the Saint's home Maderno's Baroque façade 'like mask before an ancient face'.

Santa Croce in Gerusalemme

Founded by Helena, mother of Constantine the Great, by converting rooms in her palace. Romanesque bell-tower, eighteenth-century façade with pleasing convex centre and concave sides.

San Martino ai Monti

Church founded in the fourth century; rebuilt in the ninth. Elaborately redecorated in 1650. Headquarters of the Carmelite Order in Rome.

SS. Quattro Coronati

Built in the ninth century, became a fortified church in the Middle Ages.

SS. Quattro Coronati

The cloisters. The 'lion' fountain brought from the atrium.

decline in Rome overtook even so memorable an edifice as Santa Croce. During Pope Urban V's (1362-70) short-lived attempt to restore the papal court to Rome he renovated the church of the Holy Cross and gave the monastery to the Carthusians, from whom it passed to the Cistertians, the present occupiers.

The Eighteenth Century

In 1744 Benedict XIV raised the existing façade, a pleasing example of the less exuberant Baroque, with its convex centre and concave sides. The portico was replaced by an oval space surmounted by a cupola upon rectangular piers, each with an ancient granite column before it. A corridor surrounds the oval and gives entrance to the chapel of the Crucifixion on the left and on the right hand to Pope Lucius' bell-tower, now partly concealed by the façade. The statues on the balustrade are those of the four Evangelists, with the Emperor Constantine at one extremity and St Helena at the other.

The decoration of the interior of the basilica is akin to that of many Italian churches in the eighteenth century. The vault bears the coat-of-arms of Benedict XIV and paintings by Giacinto. The conch of the apse is covered by a huge fresco in the style of Pinturicchio illustrating the Finding and the Glorification of the True Cross. This dates from the close of the fifteenth century when portions of the cross were discovered walled up in a recess above the apse to protect them, presumably, from theft or desecration at some period of danger.

Fig. 17
Santa Croce in Gerusalemme
1. Façade (1744) convex centre; concave sides.
2. Elliptical atrium with a cupola.
3. Twelfth-century romanesque bell-tower.
4. Chapel of the Crucifixion.
5. Nave with antique columns, four enclosed in pilasters.
8. Painting of Anti-pope Victor IV led to the feet of Pope Innocent II.
13. Fresco, the Finding and the Triumph of the Cross.
15. Chapel of St Helena.
17. Stairway leading up to the Chapel of the Relics.

Beneath the high altar a green basalt urn contains the body of St Cesarius and that of St Anastasius, called the Fuller, who was martyred at Salona in Yugoslavia for the crime of painting a cross upon his door.

Good Friday Devotions

From the left-hand aisle a stair leads up to the modern chapel of the relics. There, exposed beneath glass, are three fragments of the cross, two of the thorns; one of the nails. On Good Friday a bell rings and from a gallery lit with candles a priest with deacon and sub-deacon, all in red vestments, sings out in turn the nature of each relic, and blesses the people with it.

Understandably, this church has been throughout the centuries a special centre of devotion to the Passion of Christ. In an appendix to the Codex of Einsiedeln the writer describes the celebrations of Holy Week in the eighth century. On Good Friday the pope, with feet bared and carrying a relic of the cross, led his clergy from the Lateran Basilica '*ad Ecclesium Hierusalem*', there to offer it to the veneration of the people. (In the fourth century, in Jerusalem, when the people surged forward to kiss the cross it is reported that it was the deacon's task to watch that no one bit off a piece!)

The Ceremony of the Golden Rose

In the Roman Catholic liturgy the fourth Sunday in Lent is called Laetare Sunday because the first word of the introit (introductory psalm as the priest approaches the altar) is the Latin word *laetare* meaning 'rejoice' and on that day penitential observances are discarded.

It was on this Sunday that in the church of Santa Croce the charming ceremonies connected with the Golden Rose were celebrated. The pope held the rose set with diamonds in his hand during the ceremonies to symbolize the joys of the celestial garden of the mystical Jerusalem. The rose was afterwards presented to some Catholic sovereign. Included in the recipients were King Henry VI, Henry VIII, and Queen Mary of England and King James III of Scotland.

SS. QUATTRO CORONATI
Caelian Hill

The robust and complex church of the Four Crowned Martyrs[1] takes its name from four soldiers, or high officials, 'crowned' by martyrdom in the reign of the Emperor Diocletian for refusal to pay divine honours to the statues of the gods.

Until the investigations of De Rossi in the last century, uncertainty had arisen as to the identity of these saints and they had become confused with a second group who had worked in the quarries of Pannonia and suffered death under Galerius for refusal to make a statue of Aesculapius. Both groups had been buried in the catacomb *ad duos lauros*, on the Via Labicana, and both had been brought into the church by Pope Leo IV (847–55), and placed in two porphyry urns within the confession.

Although it stands upon the Caelian Hill, the basilica is at first concealed from the ascending pilgrim by the vast blind walls of the adjoining convent, dyed with the patina of the centuries, and the sense of inaccessibility is increased when the sturdy towers that once were fortified come into view. 'One enters the church through various buildings of diverse epochs.'[2] One does indeed.

The Existing Building
The existing fabric dates from Pope Leo IV, but he may well have built upon an earlier foundation and some scholars have

[1] The most satisfactory time to visit this absorbing but crepuscular church is in the early morning. Moreover, the doors are locked for the siesta with unmitigated punctuality.

[2] A. Muñoz, *Il Restuaro della basilica dei SS. Quattro Coronati in Roma*.

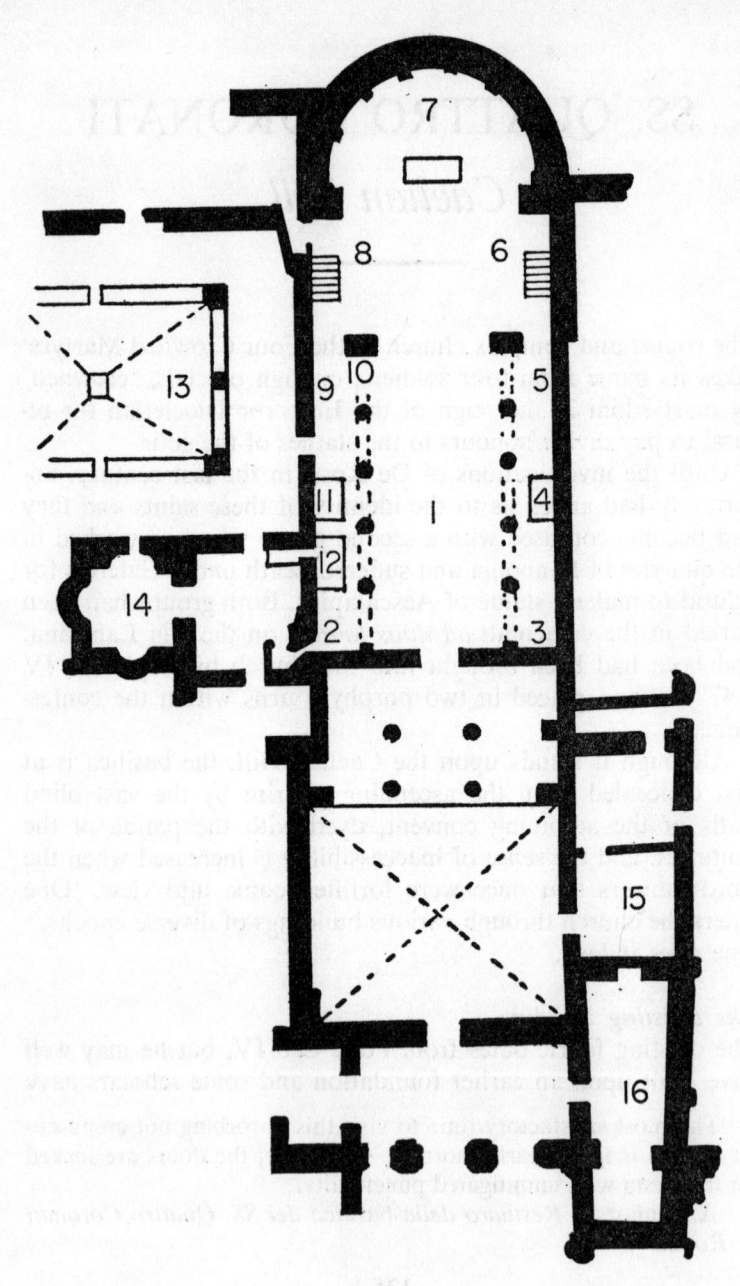

Fig. 18

thought that the first Christian edifice on the site was an oratory built by Pope St Sylvester I (314–35).

This region of the city suffered from the fires lit by Robert Guiscard's troops and Pope Paschal II (1099–1118) had to undertake fundamental repairs to Leo's church, which considerably changed its character. When the blackened aisles had been cleared away narrower ones were formed within the nave by the insertion of granite columns. A *matroneum* (women's gallery) was introduced as compensatory accommodation because the length as well as the breadth was reduced. The discarded end of the nave was left unroofed to form an open court entered from the old atrium, as it is today.

During all these happenings the porphyry urns had been undisturbed in the confession and Pope Paschal contented himself with providing a new front grille with marble side-slabs inscribed with the martyrs' names. These slabs are now in the nave of the basilica.

The Twelfth-century Cloister

In the late twelfth century church and monastery came into the hands of the Benedictines, who built the existing cloisters. The upper gallery was added long afterwards when Augustinian nuns had replaced the monks.

The charming fountain with its two basins, one circular and one rectangular, and its lion's masks, was placed in the cloister

---

Fig. 18
SS. Quattro Coronati
1. The nave and aisles, reduced in size after the partial destruction of the church in the twelfth-century.
2. and 3. Votive frescoes of the fourteenth century.
4. Altar of the Blessed Sacrament.
6. Stairway to the crypt containing the martyrs' tombs.
7. High altar and bishop's throne.
11. Altar with the relic of St Sebastian's skull.
13. Thirteenth-century romanesque cloisters—with lion's-head fountain.
14. Ninth-century Chapel of St Barbara.
15. The convent enclosure.
16. Oratory of St Silvester. Important cycle of frescoes.

by Professor Muñoz who believed it to have graced the atrium of Leo IV's church.

St Barbara's Chapel

SS. Quattro Coronati possesses two free-standing chapels, one of the ninth century and one of the thirteenth. The earlier, that of St Barbara, was originally entered from the left-hand aisle but now it is entered from the cloister. Of the Byzantine-style frescoes that covered the thick walls of this splendid little building there have survived a group of the Madonna and Child and some fragments of the turreted castle in which Barbara's pagan father was said to have imprisoned his daughter before personally assisting at her execution!

The Chapel of St Sylvester

The chapel of St Sylvester, built in the thirteenth century, was attached to the monastery but is now approached from the forecourt. (The key is obtained from the convent.) This famous little shrine, 'One of the most scintillating jewels in the austere girdle [*austere cinta*] of the Santa Quattro', is a great attraction to artists. Its frescoed walls illustrate events in the lives of St Sylvester and of Constantine the Great. One intriguing panel shows the Emperor crouching in a cup-like font with the water up to his armpits while the Pope administers the sacrament of baptism assisted by four vested and tonsured clerics.

On the style of these paintings, Muñoz made the comment:

'No doubt they date to 1246, but compared to Roman paintings of the period they seem somewhat out of date. The forms are still very Byzantinesque; the folds and linaments stylized as compared to the revival of the thirteenth century.... I suggest that these frescoes are a strange note in Rome at the time and that the artist was a Benedictine monk called for the purpose from some south Italian monastery... a master of his art and one familiar with the art of miniature.'

In the same century a floor of *Opus Alexandrium* was laid in the basilica, its surface enlivened (or diversified) with inscribed

SS. QUATTRO CORONATI

slabs taken from the catacombs. These historic fragments are not unfraught with mishap for unwary feet.

The Basilica Abandoned

When another century had passed misfortunes began to follow each other until the church was abandoned and grass grew within its precincts. Pope Martin V (1417–31) began to restore it and inserted the existing coffered ceiling. Decorative changes followed, culminating in the remarkable seventeenth-century paintings of Giovanni da San Giovanni. Above the martyrdom of the Quattro Coronati in the apse he set a vast Glory of All the Saints, a composition irreverently nicknamed by the Romans the 'Coro dell' Angiolesse' on account of the female sex of the angels!

Discovery of St Sebastian's skull

From the head of the aisles curved stairways descend to a semicircular corridor. At the central point is a cell where an altar stands above the tombs of the titular martyrs. While alterations were in progress in this part of the crypt the skull of St Sebastian was discovered, enclosed in a silver casket with a lid of Oriental workmanship. The precious relic was taken into the church and is preserved in an alcove with an altar, in the left-hand aisle. The lid of the casket is in the Vatican Museum.

SAN LORENZO IN DAMASO
Palazzo Cancelleria

Within the precincts of the immense Renaissance palace of the Cancellaria, built in 1494, is found (it is indistinguishable from the palace on the outside) the church of St Lawrence in Damasus erected originally on part of a property that had belonged to Pope Damasus' father and where he had passed his own youth. In the paternal home or in a building attached to it were stored the archives of the Roman Church. Damasus enlarged this repository and added to the records the Acts of a council he had held together with his collection of papal letters. All these documents were afterwards transferred to the Lateran, then to Avignon and finally to the Vatican library.

Damasus Commisions St Jerome to Translate the New Testament
A pleasing memory connected with this scholarly centre is that of the friendship between Damasus and St Jerome who while acting as the former's secretary received the commission to re-translate the Latin version of the New Testament. The existing Latin manuscripts were full of variants; all copies had to be collated with constant reference back to the Greek, a language not then in common use.

The Church Rebuilt with Reversed Orientation
The erection of the Cancelleria Palace involved the destruction of the ancient church. It was then rebuilt with reversed orientation but without moving the tomb beneath the high altar to which Damasus' body had been conveyed from the Via Ardeatina where he had been buried. He shares his resting place with the bones of Pope St Eutychian (275–83), brought

Paolo fuori le Mura
St Paul's after the fire of 1823. Fifth-century mosaic on the Great Arch and thirteenth-century
aic in the apse.

Paolo fuori le Mura
'aul's tombstone. Ascribed by de Rossi to Constantine the Great. Now in the confession before
High Altar.

San Crisogono
Erected in the twelfth century, part alongside and in part cove[r] its fourth-century predecessor. [Ba]roque façade added in 1626.

San Nicolo in Carcere
Built into the ruins of three pa[gan] temples some of whose columns [can be] seen in the walls.

from the papal crypt where his Greek epitaph had been found. Although not a martyr, Eutychian must have been a source of inspiration to Damasus, who wrote for him one of his best-preserved eulogies. The portraits of the two pontiffs in medallions now adorn their mutual tomb.

Interior Aspect of the Church

The interior of the church comes as a surprise. After passing through an unobtrusive doorway the visitor finds himself in a double narthex flanked by two large chapels. In that on the right-hand side is a portrait of St Bridget of Sweden and a crucifix before which she had often prayed.

The plan of the church proper is almost that of a square with an apse at one side and arcades on the other three. The atmosphere is light and airy and in this pleasant but rather unmystical fane there come to mind the verses beneath Pope Pelagius' sixth-century mosaic in the church of San Lorenzo fuori le Mura: 'It is but just, oh Levite, that light should enter your temples.'

Michelangelo's Chosen Retreat

Before the destruction of the original church it had been a chosen retreat of Michelangelo's when feeling more than usually troubled in spirit. He bitterly regretted the loss of the ancient marbles and columns and was never reconciled to the metamorphosis.

SAN PAOLO FUORI LE MURA
Via Ostia

After he built the Lateran basilica and that of St Peter, Constantine the Great turned his attention to the tomb of St Paul. This was situated along the road to Ostia at the second milestone from the city gate and a hundred Roman feet from the highway.

The modern Via Ostiense follows the same route as that of St Paul as he was led out to execution by the sword, his Roman citizenship protecting him from the indignities of crucifixion. Leaving Rome by the Porta San Paolo, it passes the pyramid-tomb of Caius Cestius, a tribune who died twenty years before the Christian era. St Paul must have seen this pyramid with its then-gleaming marble surface. His was a long walk on that hot June day, to a marshy region called Acquae Salviae, now known as Tre Fontane, passing, as he trudged along, the spot where his weary limbs were soon to lie.

The Burial of St Paul
After the martyrdom, the body was claimed by fellow Christians (that was permitted by law) and carried back towards the city to be interred in ground that was already in use for a few *columbaria* (crypts for sepulchral urns) and was later developed into a Christian cemetery.

The monument distinguishing the grave probably took the form of a little edifice, a *cella memoria*, common in antiquity. When the Christian priest, Caius, was writing about it to the Montanist, Proclus, around the year 200, he called it a 'trophy', with the same meaning as a memorial.

To build a large church above St Paul's grave was difficult, for a secondary road running parallel with the Ostian Way was on the western side, towards the Tiber. This constricted the site; and as the emperor evidently did not feel inclined to duplicate his intrepid action and build regardless of obstructions (as he had done around the grave of St Peter) the first St Paul's was a comparatively small building with its façade to the main road and its apse at the west end.

Constantine's Basilica Replaced

Before the close of the century Constantine's church could not contain the pilgrims to such a major shrine and the reigning Augustii, Valentinian II, Theodosius, and Arcadius decided to rebuild on a scale that should equal, if not surpass, the dimensions of St Peter's. With this intention the orientation was reversed and a vast nave run out in the direction of the river, an operation that involved building over a large part of the cemetery and the destruction of the secondary road.

On November 18th in the year 390 Pope Siricius consecrated this splendid edifice.

The Saracens Sack St Paul's

Twenty years after the dedication Alaric's Goths descended upon Rome and the myth of the city's impregnability was shattered. But, thanks to its outlying position, St Paul's on the Ostian Way was for a time unmolested and the Spanish poet, Prudentius, could still praise the beauty of the interior and its sumptuous furnishings.

This immunity could not be lasting and with 'the manifold procession of the centuries' came disasters by fire, by flood, and by the hands of human despoilers. In 846 the Saracens, sailing unhindered up the Tiber, disembarked and sacked the great church at their leisure. To prevent a recurrence of this sacrilege Pope John VIII (872–82) raised a wall around the basilica and its monastery and earthed-in the whole area of the tomb, which until that time had been accessible to pilgrims, allowing them a close approach.

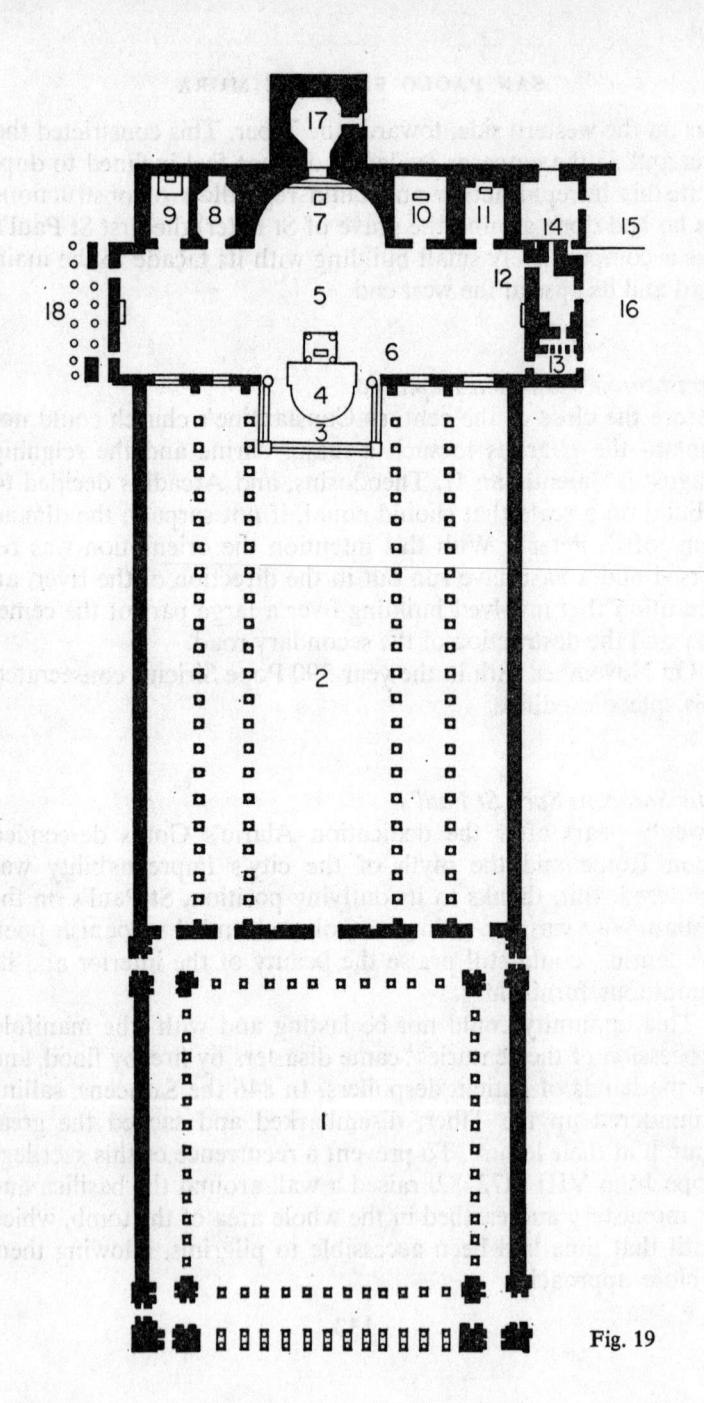

Fig. 19

The Fire of 1823

Like a great ship, the basilica battled with the waves of history, its fortunes rising or falling, but surviving without ultimate disaster until the night of July 15, 1823, when a fire caused by the carelessness of men repairing the roof destroyed two-thirds of the whole building. Providentially, the sanctuary end and the great arch of the tribune escaped with only partial injury and the shrine beneath its beautiful Gothic canopy was safe. The mosaic in the apse is a work of Byzantine artists summoned from Venice by Pope Honorius III (1216–27), whose minute figure can be seen kissing the foot of Christ as he sits enthroned between St Peter and St Andrew, St Paul and St Luke.

The Empress Galla Placidia's fifth-century mosaic upon the arch was badly calcined and in the past centuries had been restored several times so that it is difficult to assess how closely the existing composition records the original, but it is probably safe to say that the Four-and-Twenty Elders adoring Christ had made here their first appearance in the monumental art of the West.

To the good fortune of posterity, it was decided to rebuild on the ancient plan, even to the porticoed atrium.

Decorative changes were inevitable and the fluted columns that had sustained the arcading in the nave are replaced by solid granite columns. A coffered and gilded ceiling succeeded

---

Fig. 19
San Paolo
Plan of Existing Basilica
Rebuilt on original plan incorporating some of the original fabric.
1. Porticoed entrance and atrium.
3. Triumphal arch, with fifth-century mosaic.
4. St Paul's tomb-place under Arnolfo di Cambio's gothic canopy, A.D. 1385 (signed).
6. Paschal candlestick, twelfth century.
7. Thirteenth-century apsidal mosaic—Christ Enthroned.
15. Eleventh-century bronze door.
16. Cloisters.

the timber roof and the floor was relaid, magnificently, with *opus sectile* (marble inlay, often cut in roundels from ancient columns).

The Condition of the Tomb

At the rebuilding in 1823 St Paul's grave was found to have been surrounded by a metal grating set into masonry. Above or around this had been placed marble slabs bearing the words

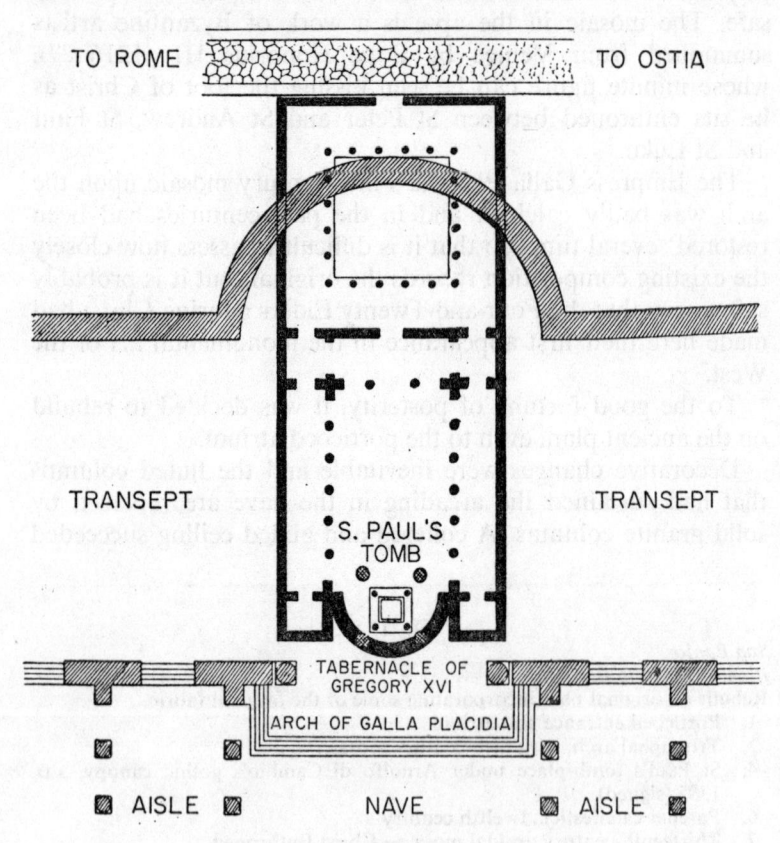

Fig. 20
Plan of Constantine's Basilica

PAOLO. APOSTOLO. MART. PAOLO upon one slab and APOSTOLO MART upon the other. As the dative form was used it has been conjectured that the inscription might have been completed originally with the name of the donor. While some authorities think that these marbles were set in place in the time of the three Emperors *c.* 390, the greatest expert in Early Christian calligraphy, M. de Rossi, did not hesitate to assign them to Constantine the Great.

Today, it is again possible to enter the Open Confession on the western side of the high altar and when the *fenestella* (metal grating) is opened these precious slabs can be seen, monuments of the highest historical importance.

Close to the basilica is the Benedictine monastery and the exquisite thirteenth-century cloisters, 'alone worth a visit to Rome'. Preserved in the former are many precious fragments salvaged from the fire. These include marble columns from the nave and the base of one bearing Pope Siricius' name and the date of his consecration of the basilica; together with some forty of the famous series of papal portraits that had encircled the walls. These have served as models for the substituted copies.

Compared with St Peter's basilica, that of St Paul had until recent times been somewhat neglected by pilgrims. Less easy of access, it had lacked the warmth of the multitudinous humanity that flocks ceaselessly around the tomb of Cephas. This semi-isolation is changing rapidly. The facilities of transport; the numerous buildings arising in the vicinity, including the splendid new Collegio Beda, all bring an increasing tide of human curiosity, veneration and love. How appropriate and how characteristic was the action of Pope John XXIII when he chose the church of the Apostle to the Gentiles in which first to make known to the world his intention of summoning an Oecumenical Council.

SAN MARTINO AI MONTI
Piazza di San Martino

The handsome church of St Martin of Tours faces a small piazza that opens from the Viale del Monte Oppio. To those who seek in Rome's ancient sanctuaries monumental evidence of their Christian faith, this church is a rewarding one; it has also been one of the most intriguing to the archaeologists.

The nucleus of the existing basilica was an oratory built by Pope St Sylvester I (314–35). Until the beginning of the present century this had been confused in old records, or in the scholars' interpretation of them, with a *titulus Equitius* which was known to have existed in the district. The topographical muddle was not cleared up until a young French archaeologist, M. l'Abbé Vielliard, began his researches into the character of a neglected building overgrown with vegetation that stood alongside the basilica of San Martino. Vielliard then made the discovery that the walls of this building were those of a third-century house of which the lower part had been concealed below ground-level. In this house was a large hall constructed for Christian worship—as he believed—in the days of the persecutions, and *that* was the *titulus Equitius*.

The House-church at Dura-Europos

To find such a house-church extant had long been the dream of Christian archaeologists. Strangely enough, there came to light almost at the same time (in 1923) an assured example of the third century, not within the heart of the Roman empire, but in the far-flung garrison city of Dura-Europos, where for centuries it had been buried beneath the desert sands of Mesopotamia. But, whereas the church of the Euphrates is quite small (its walls painted with frescoes similar in theme to those in the

Roman catacombs), the hall in the Roman house could accommodate a considerable gathering.

Some modern authorities do not altogether agree with Vielliard that a hall of such a size and in such an open position, could have been used in the third century for a proscribed religion, but think that it had been converted for Christian worship in the early fourth century.[1]

Be that as it may, to descend from the crypt of the basilica to the well-preserved rooms in the House of Equitius where history becomes tangible is a thrilling and a moving experience.

To Return to the Church of San Martino

Pope Symmachus (498–514) replaced the oratory with a formal basilica which he dedicated in the names of St Sylvester and St Martin, whose name as patron has alone survived.

Born in Pannonia (now Hungary), Martin was serving in the army at Amiens when he encountered the beggar with whom he shared his cloak and in the night had a dream in which Christ appeared wearing the halved garment. The son of pagan parents, he had been attracted to the Christian religion from boyhood and after his vision of Christ he received instruction and was baptized. Although he did not die a violent death he was called upon to endure great sufferings and was flogged under the Arian Emperors for his opposition to their heresy.

For his outstanding holiness of life St Martin was made Bishop of Tours but continued his customary austerities. His tomb in that city was a centre of pilgrimage until its destruction in the French Revolution.

Symmachus' Church Rebuilt

In the ninth century Symmachus' church was rebuilt from the foundations (*ab imis*) by Pope Sergius II. On one side of the stair that leads to the crypt is his marble tablet, inscribed with

---

[1] J. B. Ward Perkins, *Constantine and the Origins of the Christian Basilica*.

the names, many of them of women, of those whose relics he had brought into security from the catacombs.

Sergius was succeeded in the papacy by Pope Leo IV, who adorned the walls with frescoes and the apse with mosaics, setting beneath the latter metrical lines to inform posterity that he had given the church and its monastery to the Benedictines that they might sing psalms to the praise of God without interruption.

Headquarters of the Carmelite Order

In the thirteenth century the Carmelites took over the property and it is still their headquarters in Rome.

At some period the church floor was repaired with slabs from the catacombs and upon one slab was the name of Pope Damasus' famous calligrapher, *Furius Dionysius Philocalus*, whose skill in lettering would have delighted Eric Gill.

In 1650, the General of the Order, Antonio Filippini, began elaborate and extensive alterations. Above the marble columns in the nave he imposed heavy entablatures and above the entablatures formed balconied windows which he interset with life-size statues of the popes. This arrangement dwarfs the true proportion of the colonnades, causing them to look burdened.

More attractive are the landscapes in the right-hand aisle where they form the background to episodes in the life of Elias, the alleged founder of the Carmelites. In the left-hand aisle are two paintings of historical importance; the interior of Old St Peter's and that of the Lateran Basilica before the changes wrought by Borromini.

Four Popes Buried Here

Beneath the high altar are the bodies of four popes: St Soter (165–74), who condemned the Montanists (they taught the need for excessive austerities in expectation of the immediate return of Christ); St Stephen (254–57), a vigorous opponent of those who would rebaptize converted heretics; Innocent I (401–17), a firm upholder of papal supremacy and of the celibacy of the clergy; Martin I (649–55), the last of the popes to be venerated

SAN MARTINO AI MONTI

as a martyr. His 'crime' was to have denounced a doctrinal decree of the Emperor Constans II in which he set the Monothelite heresy (only one Will in Christ) on a level with Catholic doctrine.

Arrested in his cathedral, Pope Martin was sent by sea to Constantinople, deprived of food on the journey and even forbidden to wash. After a mock trial he was banished to the Crimea where he died of privations.

In this holy place there is indeed much to remind the pilgrim that 'The blood of the martyrs is the seed of the Church'.

SANT' EUSEBIO
Piazza Vittore Emmanuele

One record states that St Eusebius, priest and martyr, was starved to death in his own house by order of the Arian Emperor Constantius. A less dramatic version has it that after seven months of confinement in a small room the saint 'fell asleep in the Lord'. Actually, very little is known of his history except for the fact that he was a Roman priest and much venerated after his death.

Explorations carried out by Professor Krautheimer revealed at the rear of the church traces of a house which might have contained a *dominicum*, and a *titulus Eusebii* is mentioned in a council held by Pope Gelasius in the fifth century.

Earliest Mention of the Church
The earliest account of a church here makes reference to the need to repair the roof in the seventh century. The fabric seems to have been rebuilt by Pope Gregory IX (1227–41), and his epigraph in the porch states that he associated the name of St Vincent with that of St Eusebius. Also that he granted an Extraordinary Indulgence to all who should visit the church at any time from Ash Wednesday to Low Sunday.

Changes in the Eighteenth Century
Armellini called Sant' Eusebio 'One of the most renowned [*insigni*] Christian monuments of the Esquiline'. Whatever its past dignities, the eighteenth century wiped out all traces of ancient and of medieval character except that the ghost of an atrium might be thought to linger in the open space from which a double stairway ascends to the arched portico.

The façade faces the northern angle of the populous Piazza

SANT' EUSEBIO

Vittore Emmanuele where everything that is conceivably edible fills the huge and clamorous market. This is not without a touch of irony if the statement is true that the martyr was starved to death here.

Before the advent of the market the ground was occupied by the vineyards of the Jesuit Fathers, to whom Pope Leo XII (1823–29) gave the church and its residence for use as a House of Retreats and here many famous men came to 'make' (as the practice was called) the spiritual exercises compiled by St Ignatius of Loyola.

The Interior of the Church

The portico opens to a nave with an arcade of four bays on either side, beneath tall windows. The high altar is encompassed (the adjective seems appropriate) by substantial columns elbowing one another. Behind the altar are some choir stalls of a design that is rare in Rome. Another exceptional feature and one surprisingly in accord with the modern trend is the provision of seating for the congregation on either side of the sanctuary, thus rendering participation in the liturgy easy and intimate.

When the whole of the church of Sant' Eusebio has been cleaned and painted its architectural features will be seen to better advantage. But the general impression on the mind of the average visitor will probably remain that of a homely-featured fane, devotional and well suited to its environment.

SAN NICOLO IN CARCERE
Via de Mare

Just as some saints are hardly remembered, so others enjoy an almost disproportionate popularity throughout the centuries. To this class belongs St Nicholas of Bari, in whose name almost countless churches, chapels and oratories have been dedicated in Italy. Still greater was his fame in Russia, where he shared the patronage of that country with St Andrew. In medieval England his churches stood (and stand) in numerous sea-ports, and his chapels on many an eminence facing out to sea.

Born in the fourth century at Patara in Asia Minor, St Nicholas became the first bishop of Myra, where he died and was buried. He is believed to have been present at the Council of Nicea and to have taken part in the condemnation of the heretical Arius. His fame spread widely, and his tomb became a centre of pilgrimage. When the Saracens took possession of Myra, his relics were secretly removed to Bari, in Italy, where the veneration continued and increased.

St Nicholas Becomes Santa Claus
Of the many anecdotes concerning St Nicholas' generosity to the poor, the best known is that of his providing marriage portions for three dowerless maidens. This gave rise to the familiar figure of the good bishop holding three golden balls (patron of pawnbrokers?). But how this normal saint came to be transformed into the Father Christmas of America and England is strange. It has been said that the Dutch Protestants began the process of taking the 'sting' out of his Catholicity while retaining him as a popular figure for children.

The somewhat ambiguous title of the church, St Nicholas in

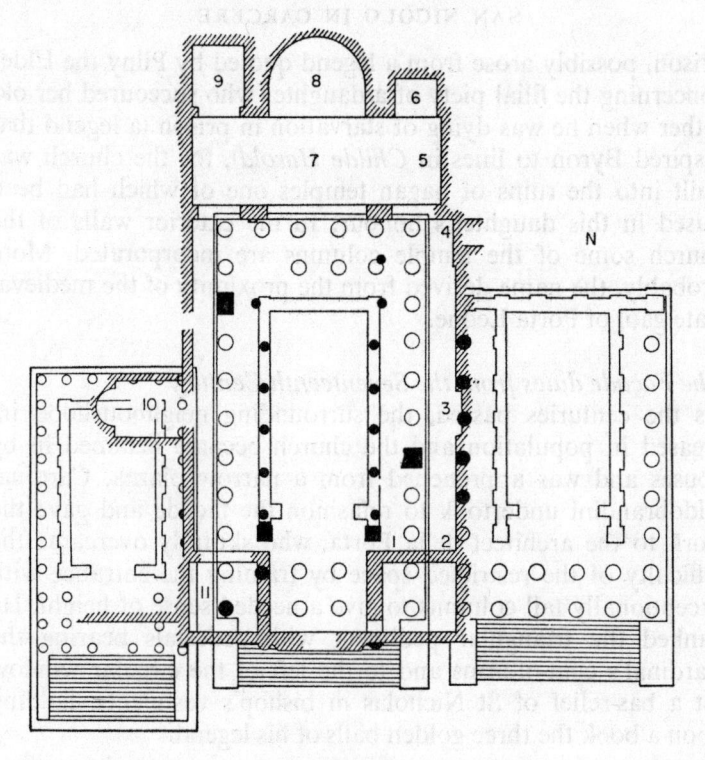

Fig. 21

San Nicolo in Carcere

The plan shows the church erected upon and between the ruins of pagan temples, some of whose columns are visible in the walls.
1. Inscription commemorating dedication of the church to St Nicholas on May 12, 1128.
2. An amusing inscription in the time of Pope Urban II of the gifts (including mules, swine and sheep) of a church steward named Anastasius.
3. Altar of the Crucifix, with a reliquary of the Precious Blood.
4. Side entrance, fifteenth-century gothic portal.
6. The Aldobrandini Chapel.
8. In the apse a painting (period piece) with Pope Pius IX kneeling in a symbolic ship.
9. Chapel of St Nicholas.
11. Baptistery, two Doric columns embedded in the right-hand wall.

SAN NICOLO IN CARCERE

Prison, possibly arose from a legend quoted by Pliny the Elder concerning the filial piety of a daughter who succoured her old father when he was dying of starvation in prison (a legend that inspired Byron to lines in *Childe Harold*), for the church was built into the ruins of pagan temples one of which had been raised in this daughter's honour. In the exterior walls of the church some of the temple columns are incorporated. More probably, the name derived from the proximity of the medieval state gaol of Porta Leone.

The Façade dates from the Seventeenth Century
As the centuries passed, the surrounding neighbourhood increased in population and the church became hemmed in by houses and was approached from a narrow piazza. Cardinal Aldobrandini undertook to refashion the façade and gave the work to the architect della Porta, who skilfully overcame the difficulty of the restricted space by framing the entrance with exceptionally tall columns to give a needed sense of height. He flanked the triangular pediment with pedestals bearing the Cardinal's coat-of-arms and to the left of the circular window set a bas-relief of St Nicholas in bishop's vestments, holding upon a book the three golden balls of his legend.

The Interior, in Nineteenth-century Guise
The interior retains its ancient form in nineteenth-century guise. The columns in the nave, some granite, some marble, had been collected from various sources. On the second column on the right-hand side an amusing medieval inscription lists the gifts to the church of a steward named Anastasius: 'Two yoke of oxen, five mules, thirty sheep, ten swine, and twenty-seven pounds of copper.' No mean gift.

Above the columns are frescoes depicting episodes in the life of St Nicholas. These form an instructive commentary on the culture and art of the age and the large painting in the apse is a 'period piece' of considerable interest. This represents the Church triumphant in heaven and the Church militant on earth. In the latter Pope Pius IX is seen kneeling in a ship (the mystical 'navicella di S. Pietro', i.e. the Church) adoring a chalice containing the blood of the Lamb. The pontiff is accompanied by bishops and other dignitaries, contemporary portraits.

Beneath this bizarre composition the undaunted artist Pasqualoni gives his conception of the Council of Nicea. In the centre, supported by the papal legates Vincens and Vitus, St Nicholas is hurling anathema against Arius. In the wings, so to say, are Eusebius of Caesarea and Eusebius of Nicomedia; St Athanasius, and the Emperor Constantine the Great.

Saints Honoured in the Church

In a green porphyry urn beneath the altar are the relics of the brothers Saints Faustinus and Simplicius and of their sister, Beatrice, who recovered their bodies from the Tiber and buried them in the suburban cemetery of Generosa. A few months later she, too, suffered martyrdom. In the last century de Rossi discovered the little basilica with which Pope Damasus (366–84) had covered their grave.

According to Armellini, Beatrice's name should be written *Viatrice*. B and V were often used indiscriminately but the two names are distinct: *viatrix* has a specifically Christian meaning being the feminine of *viator* (wayfarer), all true Christians being *viatores* from earth to heaven.

The Baptism of Christ in the Crypt

When the crypt was rebuilt, comparatively recently, some twelfth-century frescoes were removed from the old crypt and, backed with linen, taken to the Vatican. In one of them, the Baptism of Christ, fishes swimming in the water illustrate Tertullian's phrase: 'We are the little fishes born of the great fish, Christ.'

Today, stripped of human habitations, San Nicola in Carcere stands gauntly facing the wide, auto-filled Via del Mare, suggestive of a giant milestone pointing backwards across the centuries.

SAN CRISOGONO
Viale Trastevere

The last of the trio of important churches situated in the Trastevere is the splendid basilica of St Chrysogonus. Built in the twelfth century by the famous Cardinal Giovanni da Crema (Apostolic Delegate in England) it partly covers and in part runs parallel to an older church of the same title.

As with the better-known basilica of San Clemente, the existence of the older building was forgotten and its discovery has proved of especial interest architecturally since it revealed how it had been formed from a hall-structure of the fourth century converted from a third-century house. It was also important on account of some well-preserved frescoes on the walls of the crypt made by Pope Gregory III (731–41) for the housing of martyrs' relics.

Gregory was a vigorous opponent of iconoclastic vandalism and broke off relations with the court of Constantinople in protest against the emperor's heresy and destruction of sacred images.

St Chrysogonus in Tunic and Pallium
One of the frescoes represents St Chrysogonus dressed in tunic and *pallium* in conversation with St Rufo, the governor of his prison, whom he converted. Although St Chrysogonus is mentioned in the canon of the Mass, there is not very much known about his history beyond the fact that he was a Roman official and suffered his martyrdom in Aquileia under Diocletian. Another fine portrait is that of St Anastasia, her head and shoulders covered by the *palla* (woollen cloak) marked on the front with a cross, the sign of her dedication to God. She suffered in the same persecution.

SAN CRISOGONO

A Monastery Built for Refugee Monks from Syracuse

Pope Gregory showed practical sympathy with the human victims of iconoclasm and built close to the church a monastery to which he invited monks from Syracuse who brought with them their Greek liturgy and their Greek traditions in art, together with the cult of many Eastern saints henceforth to be venerated with those of Rome.

In those days the monasteries, where kings and popes were educated, were not only seats of learning themselves but also centres whence learning was spread abroad. St Bede in England; St Boniface in Germany; St John Damascene in the Orient and many others were 'lighthouses' from which streamed civilizing forces in the East and in the West.

With the refugees from Syracuse had come a boy of twelve years, for the iconoclasts not only confiscated the possessions of the Church in Sisly and Calabria, but imposed insupportable taxes *per capita*, not exempting children. This boy completed his education in the monastery and became the future Pope Stephen III (768–72). It was in his papacy that the right of electing popes was taken from the laity and reserved to cardinals, priests and deacons.

The Twelfth-century Church

As stated above, Cardinal da Crema sited the new church above the old one, whose decay had been caused by the repeated overflowings of the Tiber, which not only brought humidity but changed the level of the soil. To the new building all removable assets, columns and marble furnishings were carried up and re-used. At the same time a Bull of Pope Callistus II (1119–24) confirmed to the Cardinal, and to his successors in the title, the privileges of the original foundation. On August 17, 1127, the Bishop of Porto, within whose jurisdiction the Trastevere lay, consecrated the high altar. An inscription on the pilaster of the triumphal arch confirms the consecration and gives a list of the relics preserved within it.

Later Changes
In the sixteenth century the marble furnishings were swept away and the medieval altar now stands beneath an elaborate baldachin of Bernini's. Of the paintings in the tribune nothing remains but a mosaic in the drum of the apse, said to have been an early work of Cavallini's. The composition depicts a rather attenuated figure of St Chrysogonus, now wearing a cuirass and girt with a sword, standing to one side of the Madonna and Child. An equally attenuated St James completes the group.

A century later the architect Soria covered the aisles with groined cross-vaulting and the nave with a richly coffered ceiling having in its centre an oval canvas painted by Guercino representing St Chrysogonus in glory. This painting is believed to have been stolen and to have found its way to England; but who stole it, or when, nobody knows, nor whether it was the original or a copy that came to England.

The Carmel Festivities of 'Noi Altri'
The normal atmosphere of the basilica is one of garnered serenity but during the popular Festa di Trastevere it is the centre and hub of joyful festivity. On the eve of the Feast of Our Lady of Mount Carmel, July 16th, the people go to the small neighbouring church of Sant' Agata and fetch a life-size statue of the Madonna. This they carry in procession round half Trastevere and bring in triumph to San Crisogono, where it is set up over the altar. Early in the morning after the Octave the statue is borne in procession through the other half of the Trastevere, back to Sant' Agata.

Throughout the Carmel Feast all is *en fête*: streets illuminated, cold pork at every corner, mussels and lemons, sweets, hats, dolls, side-shows, family suppers al fresco, in brief: '*La festa di no' altri*' (*noi altri* distinguishes the inhabitants from the 'Romans' across the Tiber!).

SANTA MARIA IN VIA LATA
The Corso

The church of St Mary in 'Broad Street' was for many years a place of pilgrimage, in the belief that it had been built above the dwelling where St Paul had been a prisoner for two years in 'his own hired house'. But that is no longer thought probable. There is no mention of any connexion with St Paul until the tenth century and it is now conjectured that his place of detention would have been closer to a military station.

Superimposed Churches and Early Frescoes
As it stands today, Santa Maria in Via Lata dates only from the fifteenth century, with a façade of the seventeenth, but beneath it are two buildings of earlier date of which the upper, now serving as the crypt, has frescoes of unusual character assignable to the late ninth or to the early tenth century. One theme represents the martyrdom of St Erasmus in the presence of the Emperor Diocletian, who is seated upon a Byzantine-style throne. The prostrate martyr has extended his hands towards the emperor while two men are flaying his semi-nude body. The saint's head is encircled by a large halo and his expression is earnest but not distressed.

Known also as St Elmo, Erasmus was bishop of Formiae in the Campania and at one time was a patron-saint of sailors. The blue light given off from the masthead of a ship during a storm, caused by electrical action, was called 'St Elmo's fire', as he was thought to have the ship under his protection. Another fresco, one of the Crucifixion, has the words *Ecce tua mater* (in that order), 'Behold thy mother', addressed to St John, painted beside the cross. This recalls a statement in Vasari's Life of Cimabue:

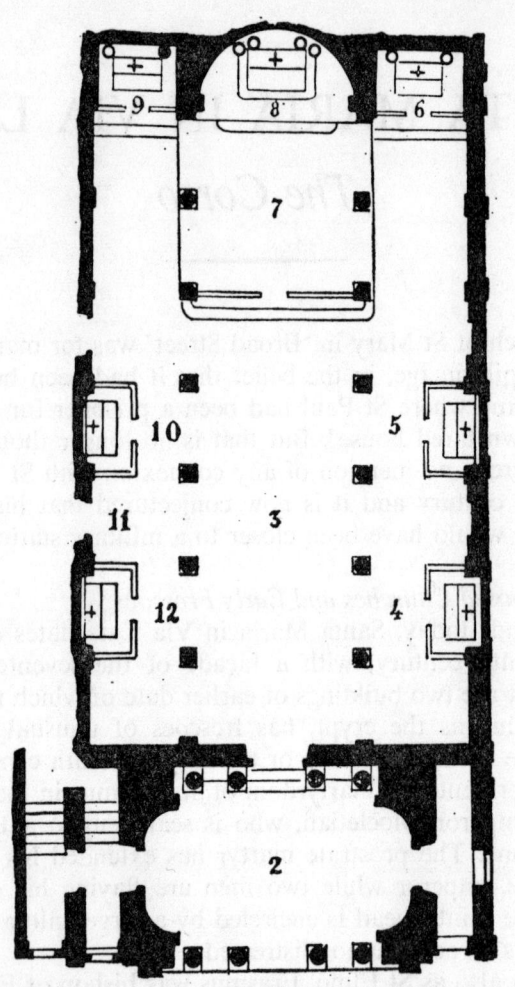

Fig. 22
Santa Maria in Via Lata
1. Handsome double porch, by Pietro da Cortona.
2. Vestibule with free-standing columns.
3. Nave divided from the aisles by antique columns covered in the sixteenth century with a layer of Sicilian jasper.
4. Altar of St Andrew.
5. Altar of St Nicholas of Bari.
6. Blessed Sacrament Chapel.
8. High altar with a famous icon of the Madonna.
10. Altar of St Paul.
11. Sacristy.

'At S. Francesco, at Pisa, there is a small picture in tempera by his hand representing Christ on the cross surrounded by some angels who are weeping and hold in their hands certain words written near the head of Christ... *Mulier, ecce filius tuua*, Woman, behold thy son, and directed to St John *Ecce mater tua*.... In this we perceive how Cimabue began to give light and open the way to inventions, bringing words, as he does here, to help his art in order to express his meaning, a curious device certainly and an innovation.'[1]

Scarcely an innovation.

Architectural Features

The handsome portico of St Mary's with its loggia (worthy of a close study) was added by the masterly hand of Pietro da Cortona by order of Pope Alexander VII (1655–67). Aligned as it is with the busy street, the façade is not seen to advantage except from the opposite side.

The interior of the church is lofty, light and pleasing and contains numerous monuments and paintings, some of the latter good. The chief artistic treasure is a lovely half-figure of the Virgin, now set within Bernini's altar-piece. This painting is 'Attributed by legend to St Luke, and by art historians to an icon painter of the eleventh century'. It is a Byzantine work, possibly later in date.

The six columns on either side of the nave are antique but have been veneered with red jasper, flecked and mottled.

Important Relics

Until its destruction in the seventeenth century, the Lenten Station for the Tuesday in Passion Week had been held in the church of St Cyriacus but when that was pulled down the Station was transferred to Santa Maria in Via Lata, as was also the major relic of the saint's skull.

Possessed of the power of healing, St Cyriacus cured the daughter of the Emperor Mazimianus of a serious illness and at

[1] G. Vasari, loc. cit.

the request of the King of Persia was permitted to travel to that country, where he also healed the Princess. On returning to Rome he was arrested (for the crime of assisting fellow Christians forced to work on the baths of Diocletian) and was put to death on the road to Ostia. He is one of the fourteen auxiliary saints[1] and is invoked against diseases of the eye and diabolical possession.

[1] Each of these fourteen 'auxiliary' saints is invoked against some particular disease.

SAN MARCELLO AL CORSO
Piazza di San Marcello

The attractive façade of the church of St Marcellus in the Corso was designed by Carlo Fontana, and completed in 1683.

Happily recessed behind its small piazza, it may be studied in comparative peace. Like many works of art ahead of their time, it received adverse criticism before it came to be accepted for the masterpiece that it is. The concave curve (giving the effect of welcoming the entrant into the church) gives the whole façade life and plasticity, i.e. it can be thought of not as a wall built laboriously stone upon stone but as one piece bent into that form by some giant hand.

In a niche on the left-hand side is a statue of Pope Marcellus; on the right-hand side, one of St Philip Benizi, a superb example of Baroque statuary. In the medallion over the doorway, St Philip is seen humbly rejecting the proffered papal diadem.

The Nucleus of the Church
The nucleus of San Marcello al Corso is said to go back to the year 308, when an oratory was opened in the house of Lucilla, widow of one Pianianus. Tradition has it that the Emperor Maxentius desecrated this oratory by ordering horses from a *catabulum* (public carriers and postilions) to be stabbed in it; and that he forced Pope Marcellus to labour there. 'Wretchedly clad and wearing a hair shirt, the venerable bishop worked in the vile service of the animals' (Pope Damasus, 366–84). Marcellus died a few years before the advent of political peace and was buried in the catacomb of Priscilla, on the Via Nomentana.

The earliest reference to the basilica that replaced the oratory dates from 418. Owing to its central position it was sufficiently important to have a baptistery standing apart, as was

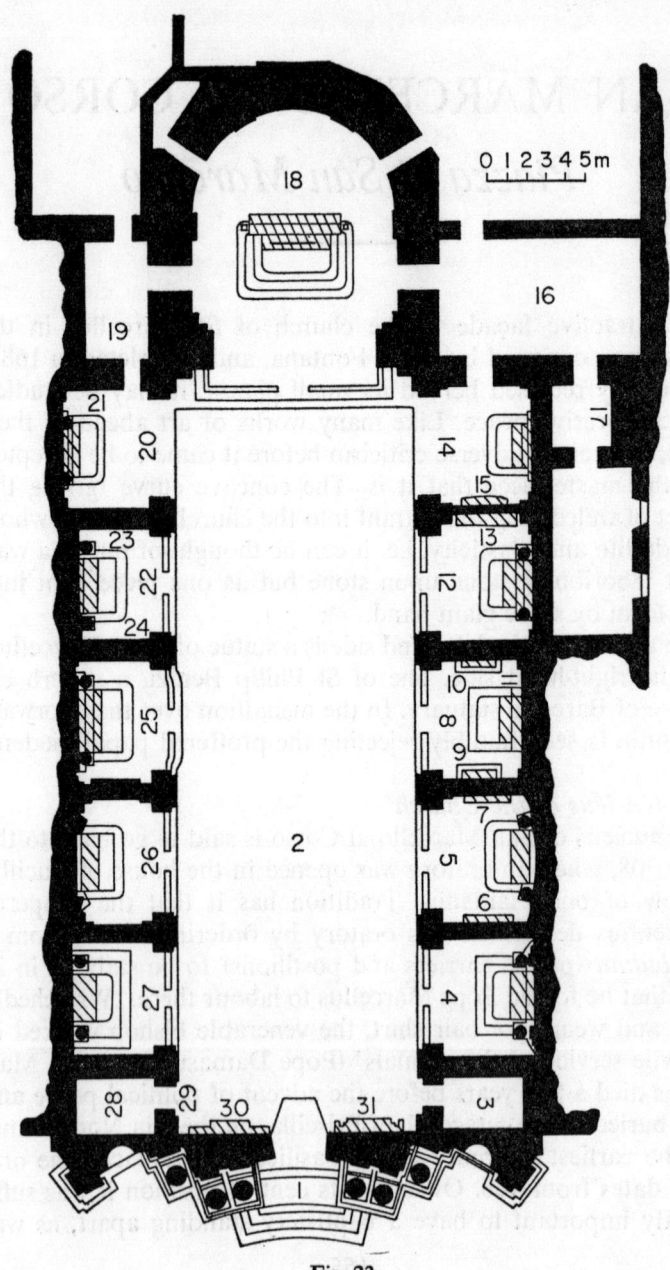

Fig. 23

the custom, from the main building. Substantial remains of the baptistery, and of its sunken font, have been uncovered at a considerable distance below street level. A covered passage and a stair now gives access to it.

Rebuilt in the Sixteenth Century

The existing basilica was built in the sixteenth century to replace the former which was almost completely gutted by fire on May 23, 1519. All that remained were the exterior walls, and a wooden crucifix found intact with its votive candle still alight. Such a prodigy so amazed the Romans that the crucifix became an object of especial veneration and in the First World War it was carried to St Peter's and placed near the Apostle's tomb while the people prayed for peace.

Rebuilding started with the plan and design of Sansovino, but owing to numerous mischances, including the Sack of Rome in 1527, it remained incomplete for many years.

Points of Interest

The wide nave is flanked by five chapels on either side, opening laterally one from the other. The third chapel on the right-hand side is of interest to English pilgrims as it contains a monument to Cardinal Weld, the first of his nation to be honoured with the Hat after the Protestant Reformation.

The fourth chapel is that of the famous Crucifix. Set above

Fig. 23
San Marcello al Corso
1. Charming baroque façade. Above the door is a bas-relief of St Filippo Benizi rejecting the proffered tiara.
2. Ceiling of the nave with symbolic attributes from the Litany of Loreto.
3. The bell-tower.
10. In the right-hand aisle, the tomb of the English Cardinal Thomas Weld.
12. Chapel of the celebrated crucifix that remained intact when the church was destroyed by fire.
16. Sacristy.
17. A Christian sarcophagus, used as a lavabo.
18. High altar.

the altar upon a background of golden stars, the dark wood stands out strikingly. Beneath the altar has been placed a *cippo* (sepulchral pillar) of the third century. This was found in the crypt, inside an altar, where it had been used as a repository for the relics of martyrs whose names are engraved on the two longer sides. The short sides have preserved their pagan military emblems, shields surmounted with crowns.

Another notable feature is the richly coffered ceiling in the nave, where motifs from the Roman Breviary and from the Litany of Loreto are illustrated in relief. This is similar to the ceiling in the church of Santa Maria in Domnica, but is a more elaborate version.

In the Possession of the Servite Order
Since the fourteenth century San Marcello has been in the possession of the Servites (Servants of Mary). This powerful Congregation was founded in Florence in 1223 by seven noble citizens, and its fame greatly extended under St Philip Benizi, renowned for his refusal of the papacy.

The Body of Pope Marcellus Found Beneath the Altar
When work was in progress in the church in 1869, the bodies of Pope Marcellus and of the martyrs, Saints Largus and Smaragdus, were unearthed beneath the altar. With them was a medal of Pope John VIII (872–82), and a lead label inscribed: CORPUS BEATI MARCELLI PP. ET. M. LARGI. ET. SMARAGDI. M ET ALIORUM (The body of blessed Marcellus Pope and Martyr. Of Largus and Smaragdus and of Others).

SANT' APOLLINARE
Piazza di San Apollinare

Thursday in Passion Week has now the distinction of possessing two stational churches: that of Sant' Apollinare, situated in a piazza of that name in the centre of modern Rome, and the church of Santa Francesca Romana near the *Forum Romanum*. Pope Gregory the Great (590–604) instituted the Lenten station at the former, and Pope Pius XI (1922–39) at the latter, with apostolic privileges, at the close of the special Holy Year of 1933. Pope Pius also honoured the church of Sant' Apollinare by reinstating in it the title of a Cardinal Deacon.

St Apollinaris was the first bishop of Ravenna, sent there by St Peter, according to tradition. He laboured chiefly in the port of Classis, where many sufferings were inflicted upon him by the pagan priests and his life, wrote St Crysologus, 'Was one long martyrdom'.

During the complicated era of the Byzantine exarchate, which held its court in the maritime city of Ravenna, several churches in Rome were dedicated in St Apollinaris' name. It was a period of peculiar difficulty for the papacy, both spiritually and financially, and it was possibly an act of policy as well as of charity when Rome recalled in this way the early connexion between the first bishop of Ravenna and the Primary See of St Peter.

The church is mentioned in the Liber Pontificalis, in the life of Pope Adrian I (772–95), who added a monastery for the Basilian monks, refugees from the persecution of Leo the Isaurian. Later it became a collegiate church and passed into the hands of St Ignatius of Loyola, founder of the Jesuits.

Rebuilt in the Eighteenth Century

In the eighteenth century it was completely rebuilt by the architect Ferdinand Fuga, and is today in the possession of the Roman College.

Fuga's church is spacious, lofty and dignified, but in design and in decoration is lacking in the verve and impulse characteristic of the Baroque at its height, and the overall impression of the interior is one of academic coldness. This sensation is increased by the unusual arrangement whereby the Blessed Sacrament is not reserved in the main building but in the vestibule which is now used as the college chapel.

A Masterpiece of Design

This vestibule-cum-chapel is, on the contrary, a little masterpiece of design. Set across the main axis of the church it is—so far as practical exigencies allow—symmetrically planned about its own axes. The general form of the plan is an elipse and it contains the charming late-Roman device of a screen of columns across each of its tiny apses. Readers may recall the frequent use of this arrangement made by the Brothers Adam.

In this chapel hangs a venerable painting of the Madonna of which it is related that when the soldiers of Charles VIII were passing through Rome, some made their camp here. To preserve the sacred picture from profanation the custodians covered it with whitewash. When the soldiery had departed and at a moment of public prayer, the obscuring element fell off, leaving the picture uninjured.

The Cult of St Apollinaris

Little as history has recorded of Ravenna's first bishop, his fame increased rather than diminished. In the port of Classis stands his splendid sixth-century basilica with its apse adorned in mosaic with a mystical representation of the Transfiguration, of exceptional charm. In the foreground the saint, vested as a bishop, stands with arms upraised in prayer, interceding for his flock.

SANT' APOLLINARE

The cult of St Apollinaris spread far beyond the Alps. In the fifth century some of his relics were carried to Rheims, and St Clothilde raised an oratory to his memory in Dijon. In the eleventh century, when his popularity had revived in the West, the Emperor Otto III built near Aix-la-Chapelle the Abbey of SS. Apollinaris and Nicholas. The devotion then passed into the Valley of the Rhine where his name, by strange anomaly, is still evoked in the thermal springs of the Apollinare-Wasser.

SANTA FRANCESCA ROMANA
Via Sacra

This renowned church, at the crown of the Via Sacra, is rich in historical and artistic associations.

Dedication in the name of St Frances of Rome dates only from her canonization in 1608. Built in the ninth century by Pope Leo IV (847–57), the church was called Santa Maria Nuova because it replaced an older 'St Mary's' in the *Forum Romanum* that had been partially destroyed by a fall of earth from the Palatine Hill.

Some authorities think that the site of Pope Leo's church incorporated a part of the porch of Hadrian's temple-complex of Venus and Rome, into which a Christian oratory had been inserted in the fourth century. This oratory is said to have been built in commemoration of St Peter's spiritual victory over the magician Simon Magus. The latter attempted to imitate the Ascension of Christ in the presence of the Emperor Nero, but fell to his death on the stones of the Via Sacra, while the Apostle knelt in prayer.

Whatever the facts, traces of an oratory were found beneath the church, and the legend has its memorial in a stone from the Sacred Way, enwalled in the nave of the basilica.

In the early twelfth century Pope Innocent II restored Leo's church and built the elegant bell-tower.

Alterations Made in the Seventeenth Century
A major alteration, no less than a transformation, came in the seventeenth century at the hands of the architect Carlo Lombardi, whose façade is a landmark in panoramic views of Rome.

The interior now resembles that of a normal Italian Baroque

San Crisogono

The grand interior. The marble columns and their capitals were brought from the earlier church. One of the finest cosmatesque (thirteenth-century) pavements in Rome.

Santa Francesca Romana

The Baroque interior. St Frances' tomb is in the confession, beneath the exceptionally high sanctuary.

Santa Maria in Via Lata
Pietro da Cortona's handsome loggia. The church stands above two earlier ones.

San Marcello al Corso
The fifth-century church was gutted by fire and rebuilt in the sixteenth century. Fontana's concave façade gives the pleasing effect

church with the exception that the side chapels number four on each side—as in the church of Sant' Eusebio—instead of the customary three or five. As in many of the city churches, the sanctuary is above the level of the nave, but here it is exceptionally raised owing to the rearrangement of St Frances' shrine. At her death in 1440 she was buried at the foot of the high altar, but when the alterations were made her body was moved and placed in the open confession. Here her statue shows her kneeling in contemplation in the company of her guardian angel, of whose presence she had been conscious for many years. The angel appears again on the coffered ceiling and upon the pediment of the façade.

Points of Interest
The mosaic in the apse has been attributed to Pope Innocent II, but some date it earlier. If the figures in their separate arches are heavy they are also arresting and the iconography suggests a blending of Roman and Byzantine influences. Probably the artist based his design upon one in an illuminated manuscript.

In the right-hand transept, a bas-relief above the tomb of Pope Gregory XI (1370–78) not infrequently raises a smile. Erected by the Senate and People of Rome, it commemorates Gregory riding into Rome beneath a canopy held by civic dignitaries. He is conducted by St Catherine of Sienna but, influenced as he may have been by her entreaties, the decision to restore the papacy to Rome had always been his own. In the clouds, a winged cherub flies over the pontifical throne, holding in one hand the tiara and in the other a very large key. Accompanied by Minerva, personifying Rome, the populace surges out from the Porta Paola to welcome the procession.

Of a different calibre is the painting, attributed to del Vaga. Here Cardinal Pole is deep in conversation with Pope Paul III (1534–49). The facial expressions are keen and intent: was the divorce of King Henry VIII the subject under discussion? In 1533 Pole had broken with Henry, and in the following year he received the red hat.

Within the decade 1950–60, an icon that had stood above

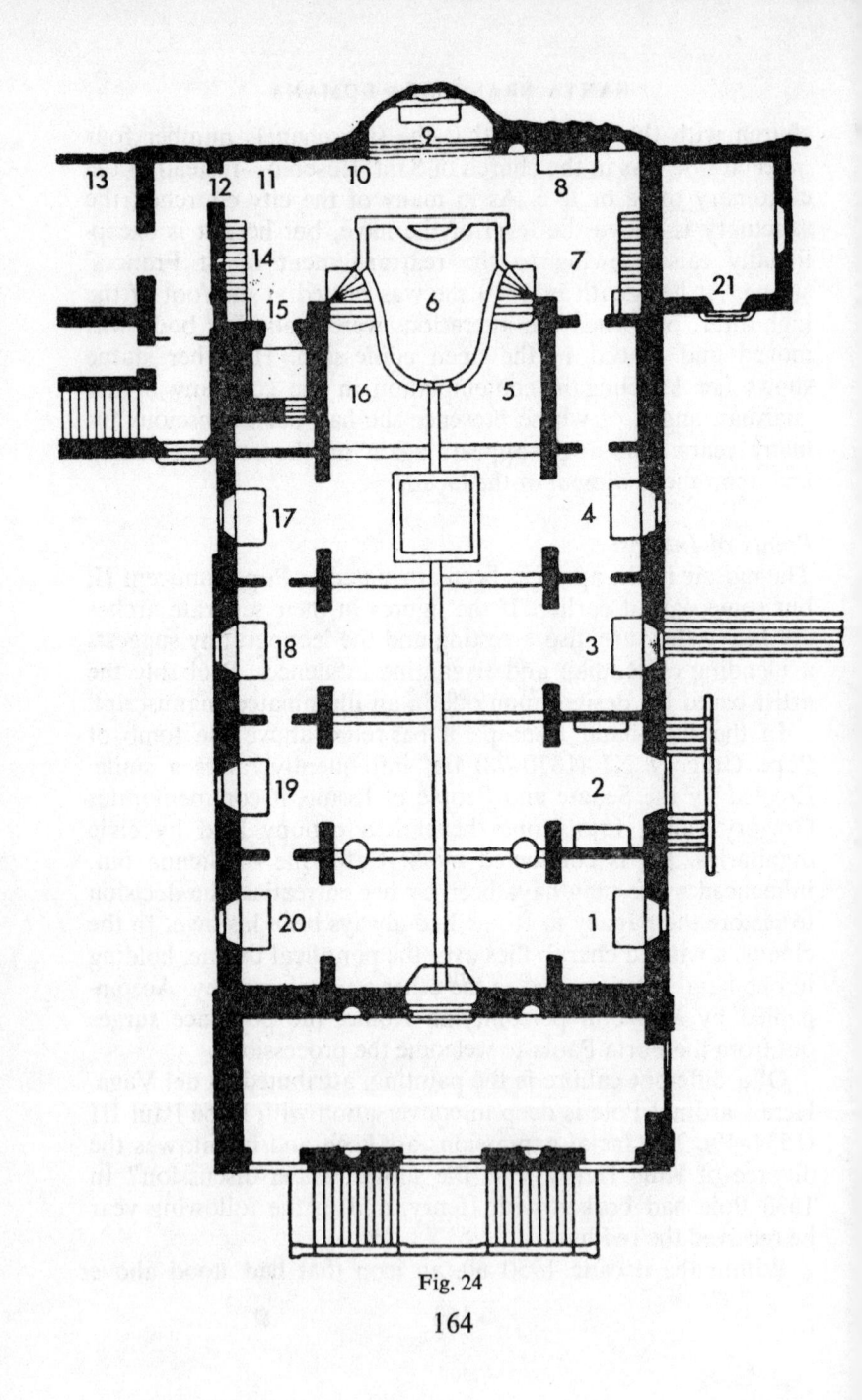

Fig. 24

the high altar was taken down and examined and found to have been over-painted. When the coating was removed there was revealed a lovely panel-painting of the Madonna and although the provenance is uncertain it could possibly, it is believed, have been brought from Troy in 1100, by Angelo Frangipane.

The Cloisters

When the Olivetans (Benedictines of the Order of Monte Oliveto) came to live in the monastery, in the fourteenth century, they built the beautiful cloisters. Renowned for their learning, their spiritual discipline and their library rich in precious manuscripts, the Community attracted many studious souls who came to dwell for short or long periods within the quietude and solitude of the house, surrounded as it then was by the ruined glories of the past. One of the last of these guests was the musician, Franz Liszt.

Alas, in 1873, the Civil Act suppressed the religious Orders; confiscating most of their property; and the happy years at Santa Francesca Romana ended. A small part of the monastery was allotted to the monks, but the cloisters were bricked-in and became the habitation of workmen and their families.

In 1900 Giacomo Boni, Director of the Office of Excavations of the Palatine and the Forum, skilfully restored the cloister with its handsome stairway, and made it into a museum for the antiquarian remains found in the region.

Fig. 24

Santa Francesca Romana
Entrance porch with Carlo Lombardi's façade—a landmark in Rome.
4. Painting of the Virgin with St Frances of Rome.
6. The open confession, containing the tomb of St Frances.
8. The tomb of Pope Gregory XI. Above it, the monument erected in 1584 by the Senate and the People of Rome.
9. Apsidal mosaic.
12. Portrait of Pope Paul III conversing with Cardinal Pole.
13. Sacristy.
21. Exterior to the church, entrance to the cloisters.

The church is still served by the Olivetans. It has been well maintained and is today a centre of vital spiritual life.

On the Feast-day of St Frances, March 9th, the nave is filled with the fragrance of spring flowers, for Santa Francesca is very dear to the hearts of her fellow Romans.

SANTO STEFANO ROTONDO
Via di Santo Stefano Rotondo

In view of the modern trend to build circular churches the vast rotunda of St Stephen, protomartyr, is of contemporary interest. When it was built by Pope Simplicius (468-83) it was also a novelty and a departure from the Christian use in Rome where circular and polygonal plans had been reserved for baptisteries and mausolea.

A Memorial to St Stephen
It would seem that Simplicius' primary intention was to raise a memory (a cenotaph) in the papal See in honour of the first Christian martyr whose cult had come to prominence after the discovery of his body by the priest Lucius near Jerusalem. As stated above, the saint's bones had been enshrined close to those of St Lawrence, in the crypt-church in the catacomb on the Via Tiburtina and to have moved them would have been illegal in the fifth century.

The plan adopted by the Pope was a fairly close copy of that of the Holy Sepulchre (known then as the Church of the Resurrection) in Jerusalem. This forged an important link with the Christian architecture of the Near East, whose influence upon Western church architecture was to increase during the next three centuries.

The Interior of the Rotunda
The interior has undergone so many changes that it is now far less complex, and less architecturally complete, than in its origin. The twenty-two granite columns upholding the central drum were probably collected from some classical ruin, but their rudely-cut Ionic capitals, some never completed, were

made for the building and the *pulvini* (blocks inserted between a capital and what it carries) are an indication of Eastern influence, as were other features now lost.

If, with the mind's eye, the interior walls are seen clothed with facings of marble, mosaics and mother-of-pearl, with which Popes John I (523–26) and Felix IV (526–30) are reported to have enriched them, this great building, now so gaunt and desolate, must have been like the king's daughter 'all glorious within'.

At some period of restoration the vast circumference was reduced. Of the concentric aisles the outer had been interrupted by four chapels so that the design was that of a Greek cross inscribed in the circle containing the walls. Of these chapels only one has survived.

An Historical Mosaic

The mosaic in the little semidome of the apse in the chapel is historically interesting. Pope Theodore I (642–49) had brought into the church the bodies of two martyrs, Saints Primus and Felician, and buried them under the altar. In the mosaic with which he commemorated them the saints stand stiffly one on either side of a jewel-studded cross. Above the cross is a bust of Christ, in an oval, and above the bust, the hand of God the Father holding the crown of life. As in the earlier mosaic in the church of Santa Pudenziana, the cross represents the one set by Constantine upon the mount of Calvary. But Theodore's cross was not a record of a great victory, but of an event that had filled Christendom with grief: the carrying off of the cross by the King of Persia in 614. Pope Theodore had passed his youth in Jerusalem and might have seen the cross on Calvary.

Frescoes Painted by the Jesuits

In the sixteenth century Pope Gregory XIII made over the rotunda of Santo Stefano to the German-Hungarian College, recently founded by St Ignatius of Loyola. The interior walls were then painted, as in the church of San Vitale, with a series of frescoes. These represented the varied forms of martyrdom

SANTO STEFANO ROTONDO

inflicted during the persecutions of the early Church and their purpose was to prepare, by emulation, the young Jesuits for the sufferings they might be called upon to endure, especially in England, Wales and Scotland. But whereas the episodes in San Vitale are unrealistic those in the Rotondo were the reverse.

Emile Mâle sums up his impressions in these terms:

'In this labyrinth of columns, thought goes round in circles. It roves (*elle erre*) from catastrophe to catastrophe, from the horrors of the persecutions to the fall of the Roman Empire, from the taking of Jerusalem by the Caliph Omar to the massacres of the wars of religion. The church of Santo Stefano Rotondo would be profoundly sad—if a church filled with the hope of Christianity could be sad.'[1]

All Roman churches have, in marked degree, their individual *ethos* and that of Santo Stefano has continued throughout the centuries to be a memorial to the agony, but also to the glory, of martyrdom.

At the time of writing this great building waits in a state of disrepair, its restoration delayed through lack of funds.

Meanwhile the Lenten station is held in the chapel of the German-Hungarian College, in the Via di San Nicola da Tolentino. From the Rector of the college permission may be obtained (apply in writing) to visit Santo Stefano Rotondo, but the permit will bear the caution: '*La visita si fa a proprio rischio*' ('A visit is made at your own risk'). It is also sometimes possible to obtain entry from the porter's lodge by the rotunda, but a book must be signed accepting personal responsibility.

[1] *Rome et ses vieilles églises.*

SAN GIOVANNI A PORTA LATINA
Via di Porta Latina

The tradition that St John the Evangelist was plunged into a cauldron of boiling oil is of great antiquity and was recorded by Tertullian, although without indication of the locality. This event, with its miraculous sequel whereby the Apostle escaped unharmed, preceded the exile to Patmos, and there may possibly be reference to it in the first chapter of the Apocalypse.

The church in Rome that commemorates this ordeal stands by the Aurelian Wall, not far from the ancient Porta Latina. It was one of the last to be included in the Stational ceremonies of Lent, and that may well have been owing to its comparatively remote situation.

Built in the Fifth Century
Parts of the exterior brickwork date from the fifth century, probably from the time of Pope Gelasius I (492–96). That there was Byzantine influence at the time of building seems indicated by the polygonal form of the apse (three-sided on the outside, semi-circular within) and by the existing traces of small vestries that closed the aisles; although these latter could belong to the restoration carried out by Pope Adrian I (772–95).

The approach is through a small piazza (the inner portion of the original atrium) graced with a cedar-tree more than a hundred years old. There, too, is a charming well-head, certainly of the time of Pope Adrian, bearing on its lip the inscription: OMNES SITIENTES VENITE AD AQUAS. EGO STEFANUS. IN NOMINE PATRIS ET FI... ('All ye who thirst, come to the waters. I, Stephen, [made this]. In the name of the Father and of the

Santa Prisca
SS. Peter and Paul acclaiming the Chi-Rho enclosed in a laurel wreath symbolizing the Resurrection of Christ, from a sarcophagus. Lamps stamped with the monogram have recently been found at St Prisca's.

Santa Prisca
Mithraeum adjacent to the Church of Santa Prisca.

San Giovanni a Porta Latina
Interior of the fifth-century nave. Note the open roof and frescoed walls.

San Giovanni a Porta Latina
The creation of the world. This fresco opens the series of Old Testament scenes painted at the top of the nave walls.

San Giovanni a Porta Latina
Detail of twelfth-century fresco of the Four and Twenty Elders offering Christ their crowns.

Son...'). Stephen, the sculptor, is the sole representative of that name preserved on such a monument.

The Portico Added in the Twelfth Century
At the close of the twelfth century the portico with its arches supported on four delicate columns was added by Pope Celestine III (1191–98). From its left side rises his bell-tower of five square stories with open arches. This tower, which expresses strength-in-beauty to an exceptional degree, seems to have 'grown' through the roof of the portico after gently displacing the tiles.

Nor are these attractions, which delay the desire to enter, yet complete; for leading from the cloister, enclosed by the church with its tower on the one side and by the seminary of the Rosminian Fathers on the other three, leading from this pleasant cloister is the entrance to a large garden. This *hortus inclusus*, where the seminarians take recreation, is in a sense symbolic; for this modern missionary college, installed with complete harmony in its ancient setting, is a spiritual seed-bed of that faith which time cannot wither; a faith that the revolving seasons renew.

The Church Interior
The interior of the church is simple and dignified, now restored to its primitive aspect and freed from the features that had falsified, with Baroque exuberance, its true character. The roof shows its open timbers; the clerestory windows have been filled with tracing in traditional geometric patterns, and the tiny windows in the side walls opened. In the apse three tall windows welcome the sun through their golden onyx, touching austerity with warmth. Ten marble columns drawn from classic sources adorn the nave. The two nearest the sanctuary are deeply fluted and of greater height than their companions, stand direct upon the floor, lacking base or plinth. All the capitals are of the Ionic order; two, of the first century, are of fine workmanship; the others have an air of decadence.

Discovery of Mural Frescoes

In the second decade of the present century came the discovery of mural paintings on the vault of the sanctuary. This led to further investigations along the walls of the nave, covered as they were at that time with lime-wash on the upper part and paintings upon canvas below. When all this had been removed some fifty episodes illustrating the Old and the New Testaments were revealed, paintings that had adorned the walls from the time of Pope Celestine. A discovery that was of major importance for the history of medieval art in Rome.

The Old Testament scenes are at the top of the walls. The series opens with the Creation of the World, a conception of fine ingenuity and technique. Next comes the Creation of Adam, and then that of Eve. All the first episodes are well preserved; the closing ones less so.

The New Testament illustrations occupy two zones. They open with the Annunciation and close with the Appearances of the Risen Christ. The Crucifixion fills a double space. Christ wears the loin-cloth; blood flows from hands and side; the feet are missing, and also the head. This had not been painted upon the plastered wall but upon a separate board the iron rivets of which are still in place. This method of emphasizing the importance of a portrait goes back to antiquity. It was used in funeral representations in Egypt, and by painters in the Christian catacombs.

As to the style of these frescoes, classical and Byzantine influences are clearly intermingled, and many of them seem unquestionably based upon illustrations in manuscripts. In the Killing of Abel the vigorous but lightly-sketched, almost dancing, figure of Cain recalls the manner of English miniaturists of approximately the same date.

The Oratory of San Giovanni in Olio

Although this church commemorates the Passion of St John in Rome, the alleged place of the immersion in oil is a stone's throw away, closer to the Porta Latina, where an elegant octagonal tempietto, l'Oratorio di San Giovanni in Olio, covers the site. This attractive little building is attributed in older guide books to Bramante, but more exact study has assigned it to Borromini. It is a remarkable indication of Borromini's versatility that he, who is generally regarded as the Italian Baroque architect *par excellence*, could also produce a work of such quiet restraint that, at first sight, it does indeed recall Bramante's style.

SANTA PRASSEDE
Via di Santa Prassede

In the church of Santa Maria in Domnica, Pope Paschal I (817–24) paid homage to the Mother of God in recompense for the dishonouring of her images by the iconoclasts. Here, in St Praxedes', he sought to honour the whole company of Christ's saints, those whose names he recorded and those, as he said, 'Known only to God'.

When he built the existing church Paschal was probably replacing a much older foundation of the same title. A stone dating from the year 491, brought to light in a cemetery on the Via Tiburtina, seems to verify this, for it came from the grave of a priest and bore the inscription: *Presbytr tituli Praxedis*. Beneath the sanctuary Paschal made a crypt designed like a horse-shoe, opening to a middle gallery, somewhat similar to Pope St Gregory's gallery leading to the tomb in Old St Peter's. To this he conveyed many bodies from the catacombs and laid them in security with his own hands (*propriis manibus*). Amongst the number were those of Pudenziana and of Praxedes, who had been buried close together in the catacomb of Priscilla.

Byzantine-style Mosaics

Monks were still fleeing to Rome from Byzantium and it seems evident that mosaicists in their company not only set the cubes for Pope Paschal but also helped in the composition of the mystical themes, portrayed in magnificent colours, with which he adorned the two arches and the apse.

Upon the triumphal arch is the Celestial City of the Apocalypse. The 'City' is an eliptical enclosure where Christ stands in the centre between angels. At a slightly lower level are ranged the Virgin Mother, St John the Baptist, St Paul, St

Praxedes, St Peter, St Andrew and the other Apostles. The prophet Elias is by the gate at one end of the city and Moses, holding aloft the Table of the Law, at the other gate. Advancing processionally to this heavenly bourne are two long files of saints, one headed by a vested bishop, the other by women wearing the veils of dedicated virgins. Beneath these two groups are a countless multitude of both sexes and all ages: 'These are they who have come out of great tribulation, whose robes have been washed in the blood of the Lamb.'

In the apse Christ descends the clouds of heaven accompanied by St Peter, St Praxedes and an unidentified cleric (St Zeno or St Valentine?) on the one side and on the other by St Paul, St Pudentiana and Pope Paschal with rectangular halo holding the model of his church.

The Chapel of St Zeno

Opening from the right-hand aisle is the minute, exquisite chapel of St Zeno. This has been called 'The one perfect work of Byzantine workmanship of the ninth century, in Rome.' The Romans call it 'The garden of paradise'. Encircling a window above the entrance are two rows of mosaic portraits. In the outer is Christ and the Apostles. At the summit of the inner, Madonna and Child are flanked by the busts of St Zeno and St Valentine, two martyrs whose bones Pope Paschal had retrieved from the catacombs (those of Valentine from a crypt on the Via Flamminia) and laid to rest in this chapel in an urn. On the stone slab where he recorded his many translations of sacred relics Paschal names Zeno 'presbyter' and a seventh-century writer calls him brother to Valentine (*frater Valentini*).[1] Upon the vault of the chapel four angels standing on celestial spheres uphold with raised arms a disc framing the head of Christ. The walls are covered with narrative or mystical themes. It was here that Paschal buried his mother, Theodora Episcopa, and her portrait is represented. As she has the halo of the living the place of entombment must have been chosen with her approval.

[1] M. Armellini, *Le Chiese di Roma*, Vol. I, p. 298.

St Charles Borromeo
When St Charles was cardinal titular of this church he built the existing façade and the archway above the long flight of steps that descend to the main entrance in the Via San Martino ai Monti. From the open atrium at the head of the steps it was his custom to distribute alms to the poor before consenting to eat his own meal. He passed many hours of prayer in the church, sometimes spending a whole night in the crypt. But he was not singular in his love for this fane of Santa Prassede and blessed as it is with the relics and the memories of so great a 'cloud of witnesses', it is in marked degree a happy place in which to linger.

> '... *peace, peace*
> *St Praxted's ever was the place for peace.*'
> R. Browning.

SANTA PRISCA
The Aventine

On the eastern face of the Aventine Hill stands the ancient church of St Prisca. Its unpretentious façade was raised in the year 1600 after the nave had been shortened by four bays.

Many legends were connected with this region. One relates that here was a grotto of Fanus and Picus with a fountain in which Numa placed wine to inebriate them; with other 'similar absurdities', as Armellini has it. Numa was the second (legendary) king of Rome and founder of the Roman religious system.

Christian Associations of the First Century
Christian associations are believed to date from the days of Aquila and Priscilla, St Paul's good friends, who lived on the hill until the edict of Claudius I expelled all Jews from Rome. A tradition that St Peter baptized converts in a spring of water here may not be unfounded although it could, not improbably, have evolved from the myth of Numa's inebriated fountain. However that may be, in the later Middle Ages there stood in the crypt of the church a marble capital that had adorned a column in the time of the Antonines. Attached to it was the (unwarranted) inscription: BACTISMU SCI PETRI (sic), 'the baptismal font of St Peter'. As the sacrament in the early centuries was administered by partial immersion, the neophytes must have crouched in the font with their knees touching their chins, like the Emperor Constantine at his baptism depicted in the thirteenth-century fresco in St Sylvester's chapel adjoining the church of SS. Quattro Coronati!

The happy dénouement of the capital's history may be seen today in the baptismal recess on the right-hand side of the nave of St Prisca's church. There, supported on the head and bulging cheeks of a Rococo cherub it is used as the basin of the font whose cover is adorned with a charming bronze group (modern) of the Baptism of Christ by St John.

The History of St Prisca, Martyr

The cult of the young girl, Prisca, was established in Rome at an early date but few details of her story have survived. It is recorded that at the age of thirteen she was exposed in the amphitheatre and subsequently beheaded. This possibly took place under Claudius II (268–70). That she was honoured as a martyr and buried in the catacomb of Priscilla on the Via Salaria is attested by the pilgrims' itineraries. A church in her name, replacing an earlier oratory, is recorded in a synod held by Pope Symmachus in 499. This building was re-roofed by Pope Adrian I in the eighth century; again restored in the eleventh it was truncated by four bays under Callistus III, in 1456.

The French Occupation

During the French occupation in 1798 considerable damage was done to the interior and when repairs were carried out the columns in the nave were encased on three sides by narrow pilasters from which the arches appear to spring. The wide sanctuary and the handsome apse were in keeping with the original dimensions. There is now a scheme afoot to restore, so far as is practical, the aspect of the fifth-century church.

Discovery of a Mithraic Temple

This quiet church has attracted more visitors since the opening to the public of a well-preserved Mithraic temple, or cave, discovered in its close vicinity. Dating from the third century, the dimensions and plan follow the norm. A niche on the right-hand side held the marble figure of Cautes (genius of morning); one on the left, the figure of Cautopates (genius of night). Cautes was found in fragments at the foot of his niche so that his statue could be recomposed and lacks only the head, hands

...ta Francesca Romana
...th-century church with seventeenth-century façade. St Frances with her Guardian Angel appears ... the Romanesque tower.

Church of Santa Prassede
Ninth-century mosaics set up by Pope Pascal I. The Pope holds a model of his church and his monogram is in the arch.

Santo Stefano Rotondo
Built in the fifth century as a cenotaph in honour of the protomartyr St Stephen. The plan was based on that of the Holy Sepulchre Church in Jerusalem.

SANTA PRISCA

and part of one arm. At the base of his supporting column is a sculptured cock, emblem of dawn. It was the function of these two genii, or deities, to assist Mithras (a god identified with the sun) at the sacrificial slaying of a bull.

The walls of the cave are painted with frescoes of male figures, bearded and wearing tunics, walking in single file towards the end recess, where Mithras is poised in vigorous attitude preparatory to slaying the victim whose upturned head has alone survived.

The figures in procession hold objects concerned with the ritual: one carries a cock; another whose virile features are striking urges forward an unwilling sheep; the fifth in the line carries with care a two-handled bowl. By his head are the words: NAMA. NICE. FOR. LEONI. Nama seems to have been used in the Mithraic liturgy as an acclamation preceding the naming of the seven grades of office, to each of which was assigned as guardian one of the seven planets. The figures in the fresco are presumably all LEONES, fulfilling the duties of that grade.

At the base of the end recess the god Oceanus is reclining in semi-recumbent posture. Water was largely used in the rite and is here flowing from a grotto to be caught in the amphora held by Oceanus. Under the group is a broken marble tablet with part of an inscription of which the existing lines, roughly translated, could read:

> 'To the unconquered sun-god Mithras
> Since often to his godhead...
> Granted fac...'

When the Christian pilgrim arrives at this church, weary though he may be, he can thrill with the knowledge that here is one more witness to his faith over paganism and, forgetting his weariness, feel 'the beauty and holiness of Rome' fill his heart, as it filled the noble heart of St Francis de Sales.

'The beauty and holiness of Rome filled his heart. Without neglecting his mission, he was more often before the altars and tombs of the martyrs than at the pontifical court. In fact he was to say to himself that the delays of Rome were providential, as they gave pilgrims time to visit the holy places and to recommend their affairs to God and his saints.'[1]

Quite recently, earthenware lamps, similar to those used in the catacombs, marked with the Chi-Rho (the Greek monogram of Christ's name), have been unearthed here. The monogram was in common use on objects of Christian art and artifice from the time of Constantine onwards and incorporated into the first, symbolic, representations of the Resurrection. On the fourth-century sarcophagus the Chi-Rho encircled with the laurel wreath is set upon a cross on Mount Calvary. St Peter and St Paul acclaim with raised hands the symbol of Christ's victory over death: *'In hoc signum vincas'* (In this sign thou shalt conquer).

[1] M. Trouncer, *The Gentleman Saint*, 1963.

BIBLIOGRAPHY

Armellini-Cecchelli   *Le Chiese di Roma dal Secolo IV al XIX.* Revised edition, 1942.
Bede, Venerable   *A History of the English Church and People.* Penguin Classics, 1955.
Berchem, M. Van and Clouzot, E.   *Mosaiques chrétiennes du IV au X siècle.* 1924.
Butler, A.   *The Lives of the Saints.* 1954.
Camillis, L. de   *Quarisma Romana.* 1960.
Cavalieri, O. F.   *Rivista di Archeologia Cristiana.* 1933.
Cecchelli, C.   *I Mosaici della Basilica di S. Maria Maggiore.* 1956.
— *San Clemente*, Series: Le Chiese di Roma Illustrate. Nos. 24–25.
— *S. Maria in Trastevere.* Ditto, Nos. 31–32.
Cecchelli-Perisco   *SS. Marcellino e Pietro.* Ditto, No. 36.
Cerdena, Jacopo di   *La Chiesa e il Monastero dei SS. Quattro Coronati in Roma.* 1950.
Chandlery, P. J.   *Pilgrim Walks in Rome.* 1924.
Coulson, J. (editor)   *The Saints. A Biographical Dictionary.* 1958.
Da Bra, Fra   *San Lorenzo fuori.* 1952.
Davis, J. G.   *The Architectural Setting of Baptism.* 1963.
Dowdall, R.   *A Short Guide to Historical Monuments in San Clemente.* 1958.
Ferrari, G.   *Early Roman Monasteries.* 1963.
Ferrura, A.   *Il Mitreo di Santa Prisca.* 1941.
Focker, T. H.   *Roman Baroque Art.* 1938.
Frothingham, A. L.   *Monuments of Christian Rome.* 1925.
Gasparini, L.   *S. Marcello al Corso.* Series: Le Chiese di Roma Illustrate, No. 16.
Golvio, V.   *San Nicolo in Carcere.* Ditto, No. 22.
Gontard, F.   *The Popes.*
Gough, M.   *The Early Christians.* 1961.

BIBLIOGRAPHY

Guarducci, M. *The Tradition of Peter in the Vatican in the Light of History and Archaeology.* 1963.
— *Le Reliquie di Pietro sotto la Confessione della Basilica Vaticana.* 1965.
Hendricks, F. *La Voce delle chiese antichissimi di Roma.* 1933.
Hertling, L. and Kirchbaum, E. *The Roman Catacombs and their Martyrs.* 1960.
Huelson, C. *Le Chiese di Roma.* 1927.
Huetter, L. and Golzio, V. *San Vitale.* Series: Le Chiese di Roma Illustrate. No. 35.
Hutton, E. *The Cosmati.* 1950.
John, Eric (editor) *The Popes. A Concise Biographical History.* 1964.
Jungent, E. *Il Titolo di San Clemente.* 1934.
Jungmans, J. A. *The Early Liturgy.* 1963.
Kirchbaum, E. *The Tombs of St Peter and St Paul.* 1959.
Krautheimer, R. *Early Christian and Byzantine Architecture.* 1965.
— *Corpus Basilicarum Christiararum Romae.* 1937.
Lanciani, R. *Pagan and Christian Rome.*
— *Ancient and Modern Rome.*
— *Wanderings in Roman Churches.*
Lavignino, E. *San Paolo.* Series: Le Chiese di Roma Illustrate. No. 12.
Mâle, É. *Rome et ses vieilles églises.* 1942.
— *L'Art Religieux du XII Siècle en France.*
Mann, H. K. *The Tombs and Portraits of the Popes.* 1928.
Marucchi, H. *Basiliques et églises de Rome.* 1909.
— *Le Catacombe Romane.* Posthumus edition, 1942.
Matt, L. von and Meer, F. Van der *St Dominic.* 1957.
Matthiae, G. *San Pietro in Vincoli.* Series: Le Chiese di Roma Illustrate. No. 54.
— *Santa Maria in Domnica.* Ditto, No. 56.
— *S. Giovani a Porta Latina.* Ditto, No. 51.
Meer, F. Van der *Augustine the Bishop.* 1961.
— *Early Christian Art.* 1957. Translation 1967.

BIBLIOGRAPHY

Montini, R. *Santa Pudenziana.* Series: Le Chiese di Roma Illustrate, No. 50.

Muñoz, A. *Il Restauro dell Basilica dei SS. Coronati in Roma.* 1914.

— *S. Pietro in Vaticano.* Series: Le Chiese di Roma Illustrate, No. 5.

— *Il Restauro di S. Giorgio al Velabro in Roma.* Ditto, No. 29.

— *San Lorenzo fuori.* 1943.

Nolan, L. *The Basilica of St Clement in Rome.* 1925.

Northcote, J. S. and Brownlow, W. R. *Roma Sotterranea.* 1879.

Oakshott, W. *The Artists of the Winchester Bible.* 1945.

Ortolani, S. *SS. Giovanni e Paolo.* Series: Le Chiese di Roma Illustrate, No. 29.

— *S. Croce in Gerusalemme.* Ditto, No. 6.

Piccolini, C. *S. Crisogono in Roma.* 1953.

Prandi, A. and Ferrari, G. *The Basilica of Saints John and Paul on the Caelian Hill.* 1958.

Santilli, P. *La Basilica dei SS. Apostoli.* Series: Le Chiese di Roma Illustrate, No. 15.

Toesca, P. *Storia dell Arte Italiana.* 1927.

Toynbee, J. M. C. *Art in Roman Britain.* 1962.

— *Art in Britain Under the Romans.* 1964.

Toynbee, J. M. C. and Ward Perkins, J. *The Shrine of St Peter.* 1956.

Vasari, G. *Lives of the Painters, Sculptors and Architects.*

Vicaire, M. H. *Saint Dominic and his times.* 1964.

Vielliard, R. *Les Origines du titre de S. Martin aux Montes.* In Rivista di Archeologia Cristiana. 1931.

Ward, Maisie *Early Christian Portrait Gallery.* 1959.

Ward Perkins, J. *Constantine and the Christian Basilica.* Papers of the British School. New Series, Vol. IX, 1954.

Wilpert, J. *La Decorazione Costantiniana della Basilica Lateranense.* Rivista di Archaeologia Cristiana. 1929.

— *Le Pitture delle Catacombe Romane.*

— *I Sarcofagi Cristiani Antichi.*

SOURCES OF ILLUSTRATIONS

Santa Sabina	Exterior, Photo: E. Richter, Rome.
	Fifth-century mosaic, Photo: Libreria Mantegazza, Rome
	Panel of fifth-century door, Photo: Libreria Mantegazza, Rome
San Giorgio in Velabro	Exterior and interior, Photo: J. Douglas
SS. Giovanni e Paolo	Exterior; brick-shaft; fresco on shaft, all by J. Douglas
San Giovanni in Laterano	Nave wall of basilica; apsidal mosaic; Photo: Rivista Di Archeologia Cristiana, G. Wilpert
Sant' Anastasia	Exterior, Photo: J. Douglas
Santa Maria Maggiore	Exterior; apsidal mosaic, Photo: Mansell
San Pietro in Vaticano	Bernini's baldachino, Photo: Mansell
Santa Maria in Domnica	Exterior, Photo: J. Douglas
	Apsidal mosaic, Photo: Mansell/Anderson
	Interior, Photo: Mansell
San Clemente	Exterior; fresco in lower basilica; Photo: Capaccini, Rome
Santa Balbina	Exterior, Photo: J. Douglas
Santa Cecilia	Exterior, Photo: Mansell
	Sanctuary with Maderno's statue of S. Cecilia, Photo: Mansell
	Apsidal mosaic, Photo: Mansell/Anderson
Santa Maria in Trastevere	Interior, Photo: Mansell
	Apsidal mosaic, Photo: Mansell/Anderson
San Vitale	Exterior, Photo: J. Douglas
SS. Marcellino e Pietro	Exterior, Photo: J. Douglas

SOURCES OF ILLUSTRATIONS

San Lorenzo fuori le Mura	Exterior, Photo: Mansell Interior, Photo: Mansell
San Marco	Interior, Photo: Mansell
Santa Pudentiana	Mansell
San Sisto Vecchio	Exterior, Photo: J. Douglas
SS. Cosma e Damiano	Exterior and mosaic, Photo: J. Douglas
San Lorenzo in Lucina	Interior, Photo: Mansell
Santa Susanna	Exterior, J. Douglas
Santa Croce in Gerusalemme	Exterior, J. Douglas
SS. Quattro Coronati	Mansell/Anderson (exterior and cloisters)
San Paolo fuori le Mura	After the fire of 1823, engraving Paranesi, 19th century. St Paul's Tombstone, Photo: Pagan and Christian Rome, R. Lanciani
San Martino ai Monti	Interior, Photo: Mansell
San Nicolo in Carcere	Exterior, Photo: J. Douglas
San Crisogono	Exterior, Photo: J. Douglas Interior, Photo: Mansell
Santa Maria in Via Lata	Exterior, Mansell
San Marcello al Corso	Exterior, Photo: J. Douglas
Santa Francesca Romana	Exterior and interior, Photo: Mansell
Santo Stefano Rotondo	Exterior, Photo: J. Douglas
San Giovanni a Porta Latina	Exterior and interior, Photo: Mansell Frescoes in the nave, Rev. Rosminian Fathers
Santa Prassede	Interior, Photo: Mansell/Anderson

SOURCES OF ILLUSTRATIONS

Santa Prisca	Mithraeum, Photo: Fr J. M. Sangiorgi, M.A., Vice-Prior in St Prisca
SS. Peter and Paul flanking the Chi-Rho	Centre of a sarcophagus, from I Sarcofagi Antichi, G. Wilpert

INDEX OF ARCHITECTS AND ARTISTS

Angelico, Fra, 60

Barbiere, Giovanni (il Guercino), 17, 150
Bernini, Gian Lorenzo, 57, 118, 150, 153
Borromini, Francesco, 6, 27, 140, 153
Bramante, Donato, 18, 57, 173

Cambio, A. di, 75
Cavallini, Pietro, 10, 75, 82, 150
Ciampelli, 86
Cimabue, Cenni di Pepo, 25, 93, 151
Cosmati, the, 29, 68
Croce, Baldassare, 118

Fontana, Carlo, 5, 47, 79
Fontana, Francesco, 30, 47, 79
Fuga, Ferdinand, 39, 74, 160

Galileo, 28
Giancento, 128
Gill, Eric, 140
Gimache, Carlo, 36
Giotto di Bondone, 25, 57, 60, 93
Giovanni da San Giovanni, 129
Guercino (see Barbieri), 17, 150

Jacobus, Fra, 21

Lapis, Vaetare, 89
Lippi, Fra Filippo, 86
Lombardi, Carlo, 162

Maderno, Carlo, 57
Maderno, Stefano, 76, 117
Massaccio, Tommaso, 69
Michelangelo, 18, 27, 31, 33, 44, 57, 131
Milani, 15
Mino, da Fiesole, 72

Parodi, G. B., 31
Pasqualoni, 147
Pietro (da Cortona), 153
Pinturicchio, B., 123
Pollaiuolo, A. and P., 31
Pontelli, Baccio, 17
Porta, Giacomo della, 146
Poussin, N., 116

Raphael, 18
Reni, Guido, 57, 116

Sangallo, G. da, 31
Sansovino (Andrea da monte San Sovino), 61, 157
Sassoferrato (Giovanni Salvi), 7

Torriti, Fra, 21, 41

Vaga, del, 163

INDEX OF SAINTS

SS. Abdon and Sennen, 97
St Agapitus, 98
St Agatha, 76, 104, 105, 106
St Agnese, 28, 98
St Alexander (with St Theodulus and St Eventius), 6
St Ambrose, 86
St Anastasia, 35–6, 148
St Anastasius, 124
St Andrew, 21, 135, 175
St Anthony of Padua, 42
St Apollinaris, 159
St Thomas Aquinas, 5
St Athanasius, 147
St Augustine of Hippo, 17–19, 24, 63, 119
St Balbina, 71–3
St Barbara, 128
St Beatrice, 147
St Bede, 149
St Benedicta, 14
St Philip Benizi, 155
St Boniface, 149
St Charles Borromeo, 176
St Bridget of Sweden, 44, 131
St Calepodius, 79
St Callistus, 78–9
St Catherine of Alexandria, 69
St Catherine of Sienna, 44, 163
St Cecilia, 74–8
St Cesarius, 124
St Chrysanthus (with Daria)
St Chrysogonus, 36, 148, 150
St Clement, 63, 67–8, 86
St Cornelius, 79

St Cosmas (with Damian) 110, 111
St Crispin, 14
St Crispinian, 44
St Crispus, 14
St Cyriacus, 153
St Cyril (with Methodius) 69
St Damian, 110, 111
St Dominic, 5, 108–9
St Erasmus (alias St Elmo), 151
St Eusebius, 142
St Eutychian, 130
St Faustinus (with Simplicius), 147
St Feliciamus, 98
St Felicity, 117–18
St Frances of Rome, 162–3
St Francis of Assisi, 23, 42
St Francis of Padua, 23
St Francis de Sales, 179
St Gabinius, 117
St Genesius, 118
St George, 9, 10
St Gervase (with Protase) 85
St Gorgonius, 90
St Helena, 24, 89, 120
St Hermes, 98
St Hippolytus, 92
St Ignatius of Antioch, 68
St Ignatius of Loyola, 68, 143, 159, 168
St James, 46, 48, 150
St Jerome, 4, 55, 150
St John the Baptist, 20, 21, 26, 42, 174, 178

INDEX OF SAINTS

St John the Evangelist, 21, 26, 42, 151, 170, 172
St John Fisher, 84
St John and St Paul, 11, 14
St Joseph, 82
St Largus (with S. Smaragdus), 158
St Lawrence, 25, 43–4, 91–3, 107, 113, 118, 167
St Luke, 135
St Marcellinus (with S. Peter), 88–91
St Marcellus, 155, 158
St Mark (Evangelist), 95
St Martin of Tours, 138–9
St Matthias, 42
St Monica, 18–19
St Nicholas (of Bari), 144, 146–147, 161
St Paphunutis, 86
St Paul, *passim*
St Paul of the Cross, 13, 15

St Peter, *passim*
St Philip, 46, 48
St Philip Benizi, 155, 158
St Primus (with S. Felician) 168
St Prisca, 178
St Quirinus, 72
St Respicius, 18
St Sebastian, 29, 31, 33, 105, 129
St Sennen (with St Abdon), 97
St Silanus, 118
St Sixtus, 107
St Stephen, 92–3, 167
St Susanna, 117
St Theodore, 111, 112
St Thomas of Canterbury, 42
St Tiburtius, 77, 90
St Trypho, 17–18
St Valentine, 175
St Valerian, 116, 142
St Vitalis, 85–6
St Zeno, 175

INDEX OF CHURCHES

Sant' Agata dei Goti, 104
Sant' Agostino, 17
Sant' Anastasia, 35
Sant' Apollinare, 159
SS. Apostoli, 46
Santa Balbina, 71
Santa Cecilia in Trastevere, 74
San Clemente, 63
SS. Cosma e Damiano, 110
San Crisogono, 140
Santa Croce in Gerusalemme, 120
Sant' Eusebio, 142
Santa Francesca Romana, 162
San Giorgio in Velabro, 8
San Giovanni in Laterano, 20
San Giovanni a Porta Latina, 170
SS. Giovanni e Paolo, 11
San Lorenzo in Damaso, 130
San Lorenzo in Lucina, 113
San Lorenzo fuori le Murá, 132
San Lorenzo in Panisperna, 43
San Marcello al Corso, 155
San Marco, 95
Santa Maria in Domnica, 60
Santa Maria Maggiore, 37
Santa Maria in Trastevere, 78
Santa Maria in Via Lata, 151
San Martino ai Monti, 138
San Nicolo in Carcere, 144
San Paolo fuori le Murá, 132
St Peter's Basilica, 49
San Pietro in Vincoli, 30
Santa Prassede, 174
Santa Prisca, 177
Santa Pudenziana, 100
Santa Sabina, 1
San Sisto Vecchio, 107
Santo Stefano Rotondo, 167
Santa Susanna, 117
San Vitale, 84

HISTORY OF MANKIND

CULTURAL AND SCIENTIFIC DEVELOPMENT

VOLUME IV

The Foundations of the Modern World, 1300–1775

LOUIS GOTTSCHALK

Assisted by Loren C. Mackinney and
Earl H. Pritchard

The Fourth volume of *The History of Mankind: Cultural and Scientific Development*, prepared under the auspices of Unesco, was planned to trace the world's cultures which developed from a stage around 1300 when mankind was largely dominated by a variety of religions in relatively isolated regions to a stage around 1775 when it was largely dominated by secular interests in increasingly interrelated regions. No significant contribution to culture, even if limited in time or area, goes unmentioned and those contributions which had entered or might enter into the global heritage of mankind are given special consideration. In addition to European achievements in culture and science, the authors have given special attention to the contributions of non-European peoples.

This book opens with a general outline of world history between the fourteenth century and 1775. Part One continues by describing the great religious, political and economic institutions which dominated the world scene during this period. Part Two, copiously illustrated, is devoted to the emergence of literature, to the development of art in its various forms, to the progress of science and technology, and to education during a period in which the foundations of the modern world gradually emerged through the late Middle Ages, the Renaissance, the age of discoveries, the Scientific Revolution, and the Enlightenment. The book provides a major survey of the history of civilization during key centuries of world development.

LONDON: GEORGE ALLEN AND UNWIN LTD

GEORGE ALLEN & UNWIN LTD

Head Office
40 Museum Street, London W.C.1
Telephone: 01-405 8577

Sales, Distribution and Accounts Departments
Park Lane, Hemel Hempstead, Herts.
Telephone: 0442 3244

Athens: 34 Panepistimiou Street
Auckland: P.O. Box 36013, Northcote Central N.4
Barbados: P.O. Box 222, Bridgetown
Beirut: Deeb Building, Jeanne d'Arc Street
Bombay: 103/5 Fort Street, Bombay 1
Buenos Aires: Escritorio 454-459, Florida 165
Calcutta: 285J Bepin Behari Ganguli Street, Calcutta 12
Cape Town: 68 Shortmarket Street
Hong Kong: 105 Wing On Mansion, 26 Hancow Road, Kowloon
Ibadan: P.O. Box 62
Karachi: Karachi Chambers, McLeod Road
Madras: 2/18 Mount Road, Madras
Mexico: Villalongin 32, Mexico 5, D.F.
Nairobi: P.O. Box 30583
Philippines: P.O. Box 157, Quezon City D-502
Rio de Janeiro: Caixa Postal 2537-Zc-00
Singapore: 36c Prinsep Street, Singapore 7
Sydney N.S.W.: Bradbury House, 55 York Street
Tokyo: C.P.O. Box 1728, Tokyo 100-91
Toronto: 81 Curlew Drive, Don Mills